SKILLS *of the* GAME

Badminton

Mark Golds

The Crowood Press

First published in 2002 by
The Crowood Press Ltd
Ramsbury, Marlborough
Wiltshire SN8 2HR

www.crowood.com

This impression 2005

British Library Cataloguing-in-Publication Data
A catalogue record for this book is available from the British Library.

ISBN 1 86126 433 X

Acknowledgements
The author would like to thank the following individuals and
organizations for their help in preparing this book: The Badminton
Association of England, Lynda Belshaw, Carlton Rackets, Alan Clarkson,
Tom Dunlop, Peter Ferns, Paul Golds, Nadia Kudiarskyj, David Lloyd
Leisure, The International Badminton Federation, Kenneth Madsen,
Monkhouse Sports, Andy Pound, Reinforced Shuttlecock Limited,
Rebecca Shaw, Emma Tyler, Caroline Williams and Harry Wright.

Special thanks to Martin Andrew, who was my nutritional expert and
whose help throughout the whole of the book was greatly appreciated.

Line drawings by Annette Findlay.

Note
All shots illustrated are shown and described for right-handed players.

Typeset by Jean Cussons Typesetting, Diss, Norfolk

Printed and bound in Great Britain by Arrowsmith, Bristol

Contents

Foreword

Mark comes from a distinguished sporting family, all of whom have been great supporters of badminton.

He was born in 1965 and is now at that enviable age at which he can draw on his vast knowledge and experience of this very popular racket sport, and, at the same time, take to the court and demonstrate the strokes and tactics at the highest level.

Over the past twenty years I have watched Mark develop from being a talented junior, representing England in international matches, to enjoying an exceptional county career representing his native Cheshire. Currently, Mark continues to play an integral part in the team's success in the Premier Division of the Inter-County Championships.

At this comparatively early stage in his coaching career he has already produced some excellent juniors who have since reached county and national ranking. Mark's enthusiasm, commitment and easy style of communication have made him a popular coach and created a demand for his services at all levels.

In the past, it was quite rare for top players to take up coaching. There seems to be a change in that trend – Mark is part of that change.

Roger Ewing
Director, Badminton Association of
England (BAofE)
Chairman, Cheshire County Badminton
Association (CCBA)

Fig 1 Mark Golds coaching juniors.

Introduction

Battledore and Shuttlecock, the forerunner of badminton, was a popular rallying game that probably originated in ancient Greece around 2,000 years ago. The game then spread to the Far East, China, Japan and India. Records show that in late sixteenth-century England, peasants were playing a rallying game. Battledore and shuttlecock was simply a game of hitting a shuttle between two people as many times as possible without it hitting the ground, and was a social outdoor pastime rather than a competitive sport.

The game of badminton dates back to 1873. Army officers, on leave from India, called it badminton as they were staying at Badminton House in Gloucestershire, home to the Duke of Beaufort. In 1875, army officers in Folkestone formed the first club, which was soon followed by other clubs in southern England. In 1893, the Badminton Association of England (BAofE) was founded when fourteen club representatives met and agreed a uniform set of rules for the game.

In 1899, the first All England Championships were held at the London-Scottish Drill Hall in Buckingham Gate. Only doubles were played and the winners were as follows:

Men's doubles	D. Oakes and S. M. Massey;
Ladies' doubles	Miss M. Lucas and Miss Graeme;
Mixed doubles	D. Oakes and Miss St. John.

Singles events followed in 1900 with the first winners being S. H. Smith and Miss E. Thomson.

During the early 1900s the game grew in popularity throughout Europe, the USA and Asia and a need arose for an international organization. In 1934, the International Badminton Federation (IBF) was formed – this standardized rules across countries. The IBF had nine founder members including England, Ireland, Scotland and Wales. This figure has now risen to 140 full member countries, which demonstrates the massive popularity of badminton worldwide.

The first international men's team competition, the Thomas Cup, presented by Sir George Thomas Bart, was held in 1949. The first ladies team competition, the Uber Cup, presented by Mrs Betty Uber, was held in 1957.

In 1979, the first individual world championships were held in Malmo, Sweden. The men's singles was won by Fleming Delfs (Denmark), the ladies singles by Lene Koppen (Denmark). Indonesia won the men's doubles, Japan the ladies doubles and Denmark the mixed doubles.

Also in 1979, badminton became an 'open' sport: the first professional tournament, the 'Masters' was held at the Royal Albert Hall in London.

In the years that followed, China emerged as a new power in badminton, soon to be followed by Korea. Records of world

Fig 2 Early version of badminton circa 1874.

championships and Grand Prix tournaments demonstrate the dominance of China and Korea during the mid-1980s. Indonesia remains a strong force, with Denmark, England and Sweden following closely.

Badminton gained Olympic status in 1992, which had a major impact on the sport as it led to a dramatic rise in standards in many countries because their national associations received an increase in funding. There are now many smaller nations beginning to take part in the sport and competing on the world stage.

Badminton is a sport that can be played by people of all ages, in groups or individually. It provides a healthy, lifelong sporting activity that is easily accessible to men, women, young people and those with a disability. The sport is very popular, played by a billion people worldwide. In England there are over 2,050 BAofE-affiliated clubs and many more unaffiliated.

Badminton is a very popular sport in schools where children may be introduced to it for the first time. Some of these children develop into outstanding athletes, playing in tournaments and matches throughout the country, and possibly, for the top few internationally.

Badminton is regarded as the fastest racket sport. The shuttle reaches speeds in excess of 240km/h (150mph) The fastest recorded hit of 260km/h (162mph) was made by Simon Archer in 1998/9. Developments in technology have increased the speed of the game as rackets are now very light. Improvements have also been made in the way top players train to get the best out of their physiques. Both of these factors have led to the fast, dynamic and powerful game we know today.

CHAPTER 1
Badminton Basics

RACKETS

Since badminton started in the early nineteenth century, the badminton racket has evolved to incorporate advances in both materials and computer knowledge.

In the illustration below, the racket on the left-hand side is an original battledore racket, which has a long, thin handle and a vellum hitting surface. Battledore played an important part in the development of both badminton and table tennis.

The racket second from the left is an Indian white racket *circa* 1880–90, possibly manufactured in India. The racket features double centre mains stringing and is of a very sturdy construction which weighs a little under 250g (9oz).

The centre racket is a Hazell's streamline *Red Star*, which is a very rare example of a Hazell's triple branch racket. The streamline rackets were invented in the mid-1930s by Frank Donisthorpe.

The racket second from the right is a 1950s laminated wood racket made up of different woods to make the racket stronger and more durable. This racket weighs 130g (4½oz) and has natural gut strings.

The racket on the far right is a Carlton graphite/titanium in which modern tech-

Fig 3 Rackets past and present.

nology has been used to maximize strength and lightness, the qualities required for today's game.

Rackets can vary in price from £10.00 to £150.00 for a top of the range model. Knowledge gained from other sports including tennis, cycling and skiing have all helped to develop the modern badminton racket.

CLOTHING

Clothing has changed from long trousers and long-sleeved shirts, as seen in Fig 2, to shorts and loose-fitting shirts, seen elsewhere in the book, which keep moisture away from the body. The shoe is a very important part of any player's equipment: it has to be light, flexible and very strong to cope with the demands of the game.

SHUTTLES

The feather shuttle, made of goose feathers, is the best to play badminton with and is used in all major championships and matches throughout the world. It has a natural flight in the air and consistency of control and feel.

The plastic shuttle was introduced to offset the high cost of the feather shuttle. The design of the plastic shuttle has greatly improved in recent years to mimic the performance of the feather shuttle, and it is far more durable.

Original shuttles were very crude in their construction, using chicken feathers stuck into uncovered cork. Around the turn of the century, shuttlecocks became more standardized and a shuttle called the 'barrel', so-called because of its shape, was very popular and used in the 1902 All England Championships.

In 1908 the barrel shuttle was replaced in the Championships by an early version of the modern-day shuttlecock. This shuttle was known as the 'straight' because the feather quills were fixed with the flat side to the inside, which resulted in the stitching straightening out the natural curve of the feathers.

Shuttles then began to be made of goose feathers, which are still accepted as the best to use. The average weight of the shuttle was approximately 80 grains, which is less than 5g (⅕oz). It is the natural oils in the shuttle that help it maintain the strength and suppleness to withstand the blows of a racket. Goose feathers contain around 10 per cent natural oils: duck feathers have less, making them more brittle and less durable.

Reinforced Shuttlecocks Ltd (RSL) were pioneers in the manufacture of shuttles in a wide range of speeds. There are thirteen different speeds in the higher grades of shuttles.

The following table shows the speeds of feather shuttles.

Slow	73, 74, 75
Slow – medium	76, 76
Medium	78, 79, 80, 81
Medium – fast	82, 83
Fast	84, 85

The speeds are numbered from 73 to 85 and represent the weight of a shuttle in grains. There are 7,000 grains to 1lb (0.45kg). As a guide, each grain adds approximately 10cm (4in) to the length of flight. Speed 77 is best used in warm halls, 78–82 are best in cooler/cold halls. However, this is only a guide and all shuttles should be tested individually before playing (see page 92 for rules governing the testing of shuttles for the correct speed).

Fig 4 Early versions of shuttles and the changes to the present day feather shuttlecock.

The storage of shuttles is important, as storing them incorrectly will lead to the shuttle drying out and becoming brittle. All feather shuttles should be stored in a slightly damp atmosphere and at a temperature not exceeding 13°C (55°F).

BADMINTON COURTS

The two court areas for playing singles and doubles are different. Note also that the doubles court (shown overleaf) has a specific service box area.

Fig 5 The singles court.

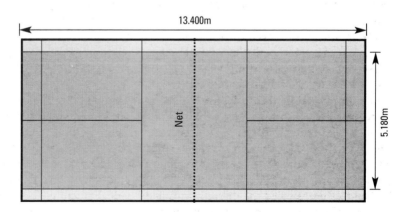

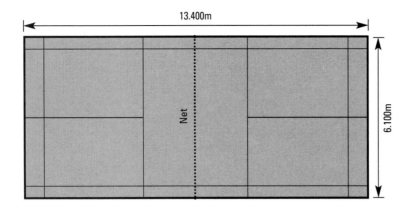

Fig 6 The doubles court.

GRIPS

Holding the racket correctly is an essential part of playing the game well and if this is not done correctly then it can lead to missing shots and wrong body positions. Getting young players to hold their racket correctly is, without a doubt, the most important thing about teaching the game. A good idea is to use objects such as balloons and air-filled paper balls: this gives the young player time to watch and correct the grip as the object falls.

As mentioned previously, more than one type of grip may need to be used during rallies, and the ability to change grip quickly is an essential part of any player's game. In between playing strokes, the player's hand around the grip should be relaxed. This will enable the player to change grip quickly and efficiently, and will allow a change of position. The player should always find a comfortable grip as this will facilitate good shot production.

BASIC SHOTS

All players should learn the following basic shots which will enable them to play the game to a high standard, whether it is singles or doubles.

Fig 7 Using a balloon is a great way to teach a young player the correct grips.

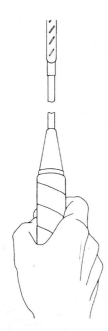

Fig 8 Basic forehand grip.

Fig 10 Universal grip.

Fig 9 Basic backhand grip.

High and Low Serve: Forehand and Backhand

(*see* Chapter 2)

Drop Shot: Forehand and Backhand

This shot is normally played from the rear court and aimed towards the opponent's forecourt. It is an overhead shot that is angled downwards, flying close to the top of the net.

Clear: Forehand and Backhand

This shot is normally played from the rear court and aimed towards the opponent's rear court. It is an overhead shot that is played high into the air.

Smash: Forehand and Backhand

This shot can be played from anywhere on the court. It is a shot that is hit overhead in such a manner that it lands in the opponent's court very quickly. It is an explosive shot that flies close to the net and can be hit with varying amounts of power.

Lift: Forehand and Backhand

This shot is normally played from the fore-court to the opponent's rear court. It is played from in front of the body and lifted above the opponent's head towards the back tramlines.

Net Shot: Forehand and Backhand

This shot is played from the forecourt to the opponent's forecourt. It is played from in front of the body and should just clear the net.

Push: Forehand and Backhand

This shot is mainly played in doubles, where one side does not wish to lift the shuttle which could then be attacked by the opponents. It is a very controlled shot, often used when the shuttle has dropped below the level of the net. A small swing with limited follow through is used when playing the push on either the backhand or forehand side.

Block: Forehand and Backhand

Block shots are played as a return to smashes and fast drop shots. They are played from the mid-court and blocked back to the opponent's forecourt. There are two types of block shot:

- tight block to the net;
- flat block landing beyond the opponent's service line.

Both of these shots are used in all types of games for varying reasons. The tight block to the net is used to bring the opponent closely in to the forecourt in singles. The flat block is used more in doubles, turning defence into attack.

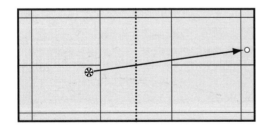

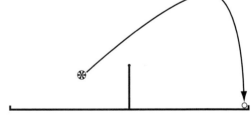

Fig 11 The high serve.

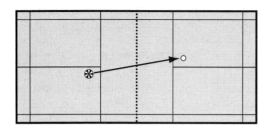

Fig 12 The low serve.

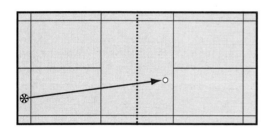
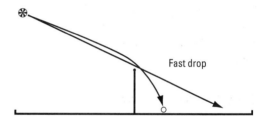

Fast drop

Fig 13 The drop shot.

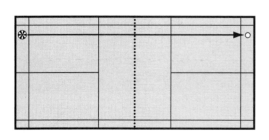
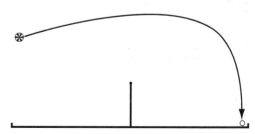

Fig 14 Backhand clear.

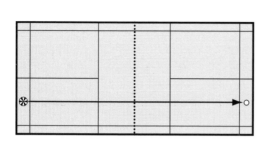

Fig 15 Forehand clear.

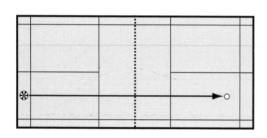

Fig 16 The smash.

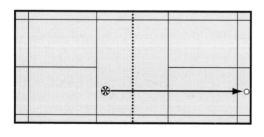

Fig 17 The lift shot.

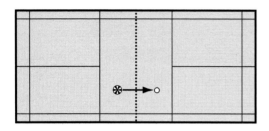 

Fig 18 The net shot.

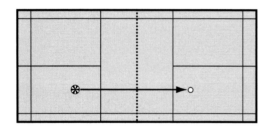 

Fig 19 The push shot.

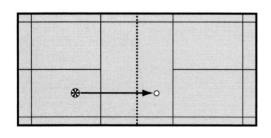 

Fig 20 The block shot.

CHAPTER 2
The Service

THE HIGH SERVE

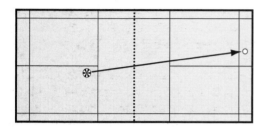

Fig 21 The high serve, overhead view.

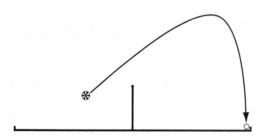

Fig 22 Flight path of the high serve.

The high serve is generally used in singles to position the opponent towards the rear of the court. The server positions himself in the service box near to the centre line and not too far away from the short service line. The server should be balanced with feet apart, standing side-on, (non-racket side nearest to the net). The racket is taken back behind the server's body with the body weight on the back foot. The shuttle is held in front and slightly to the side of the server.

Fig 23 Preparation stance for a high serve.

16

During the racket swing, the server's body weight is transferred to the front foot. The racket is powerfully swung forward to meet the falling shuttle and contact is made, lifting the shuttle up high and deep into the opponent's court. The racket swing continues diagonally upward to finish above the server's non-racket shoulder.

Coaching Tips

- Get balanced.
- Obey service laws.
- Do not try to over hit the shuttle.
- Transfer body weight to the front foot during the hit.
- Finish with a high follow through.
- Try not to slice the serve by turning the wrist during the swing.

The Flick Serve

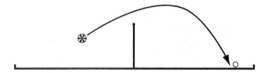

Fig 24 Flight path for a flick serve.

Flick serves are high serves but played with deception and a much flatter trajectory. The server makes the serve look like it is going to be a low serve and then at the last minute uses his wrist to powerfully flick up and lift the shuttle above and past the opponent.

The serve can be used with great effect when playing level doubles and mixed doubles, but it is a difficult serve to control and requires a lot of practice to fully master it.

THE LOW SERVE

The low serve is an attacking shot, generally used in doubles. There are forehand and backhand methods for this serve, however the majority of county and international players use a backhand low serve with a backhand grip.

Backhand

The aim of this serve is to make the shuttle skim the top of the net and land on or just over the receiver's service line, thus forcing the receiver to lift the shuttle back over the net.

The server should stand in a comfortable position with either one foot forward or both feet level, however he must not move either foot during the service action. The shuttle should be held loosely in the fingertips. The point of contact is in front of the server's body.

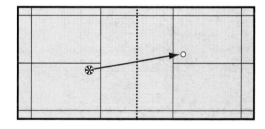

Fig 25 The low serve, overhead view.

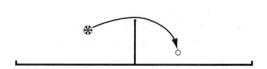

Fig 26 Flight path of a low serve.

Fig 28 *Forehand low serve position.*

Fig 27 *Backhand low serve position.*

The action for this serve is a push and not a hit, which gives added control over the shuttle. The shuttle is hit from the server's fingers, not dropped, as it would then become a moving target and more difficult to control.

Forehand

Used in both singles and doubles matches, the main aim of this serve is the same as the backhand low serve, which is to prevent the opposition attacking the shuttle by hitting down and forcing a lift return.

The arm action is a push forward using a firm wrist and bent arm. The shuttle is dropped and pushed forward towards the net, lifting the shuttle just above net level. The difficulty with this shot is the timing of

the shuttle as it drops and controlling the push action. Technically this is a difficult shot to play but, with practice, it can be played efficiently and with great effect.

Coaching Tips

- Get into a comfortable, well-balanced position.
- Do not hurry.
- The action for a low serve is a push, not a hit.
- Racket up after the serve.
- Do not drop the shuttle – hit direct from the hand.
- A shorter backhand grip is recommended as this gives more control during the serve.

CHAPTER 3
Forehand Shots

FOREHAND OVERHEAD HITTING ACTION

The basic movement for the forehand overhead hitting action may be compared with the action of throwing a ball.

The movement starts with the racket being taken back to shoulder level. As this happens, the upper body rotates in preparation to hit the shuttle. The racket is then thrown forward and upward towards the falling shuttle. As the player throws the racket head forward at the shuttle, his body should also start to move forward. Weight should be transferred to the front foot as this improves the player's recovery to a base position after the shot has been played.

Once the shuttle has been hit, the racket continues its swing and follow through. The player should try to keep his body upright and not bend down at this point.

FOREHAND SHOTS (REAR COURT)

There are three basic forehand shots that are played from the rear of the court: the drop shot, the clear and the smash. All of these shots can be broken down into three elements: preparation, execution and recovery.

The preparation for all the shots should look identical so that the opposition cannot anticipate which shot is being played.

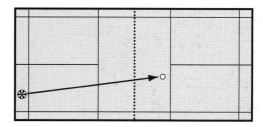

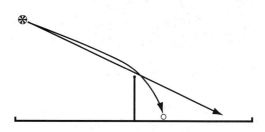

Fig 29 Flight paths for a fast and a slow drop shot.

The shot execution will vary with the speed of the racket head slice and the angle of the point of contact. The point of contact between the racket and the shuttle should be at a full but relaxed reach above the player's head and in front of the racket shoulder so that, if the shuttle was to land on the player, it would drop on to the upper part of the chest (just below the collarbone) on the racket side.

Recovery should be quick and efficient to enable the player to prepare for the next shot.

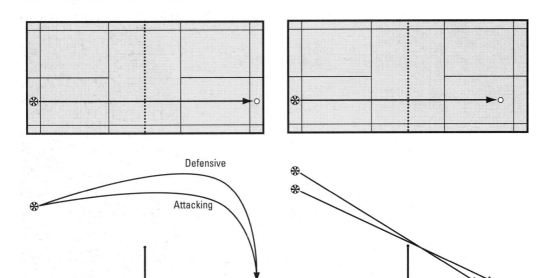

Fig 30 Flight paths for an attacking and a defensive clear.

Fig 31 Flight paths for a smash and a jump smash.

Fig 32
Preparation
position.

Fig 33 Racket and body position at point of contact for a forehand overhead shot.

These three elements, when adopted by players, will not only lead to consistency with the shots but will also create disguise and deception for clears, drops and smashes.

Fig 34 Recovery position after the shot has been played.

Drop Shot

The principle of the drop shot is to play an overhead stroke from the rear court to the opponent's forecourt with the aim of bringing the opponent close in to the net, thereby creating space in his rear court and forcing a weak return.

The fast drop, played with a quicker arm and racket action, lands deeper into the opponent's court and has a faster flight time, thereby reducing the opponent's response time.

21

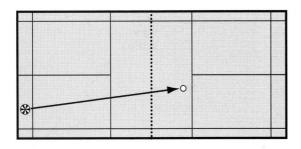

Fig 35 Flight path of a basic drop shot.

Fig 36 Flight path of a closed face drop shot.

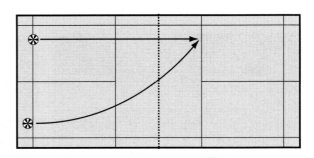

The flight path of a basic drop shot will change depending on the racket head speed at point of contact with the shuttle. The shuttle can be sliced to create angles around the court. There are two types of forehand slice: closed racket face and open racket face. The idea of slicing is to add deception to the drop shot. There are a number of ways in which a player can produce a good slice drop shot, including racket speed and racket angle at point of contact.

Coaching Tips

- Position the body behind the shuttle.
- Good footwork and early racket preparation are very important.
- Hit through the shuttle with a full swing.
- Footwork to move through the shot for full recovery to the base.

Clear

The main reason for playing a high or defensive clear is to create time for a full recovery to be made by the hitter when under pressure. The height and depth of the shuttle's flight means that it stays in the air longer, allowing more time for recovery.

An alternative to the high clear is the attacking clear, often known as the 'punch' clear. This is where the player hits the shot on a flatter trajectory, which reduces the flight time of the shuttle and consequently the time available for response from the opponent.

The build-up for this shot is exactly the same as for the drop, the smash and the normal high clear, but the shuttle is punched with the racket swing to create a flatter and faster shot which will catch the opponent unaware and without sufficient time to move to a good position to return the shot.

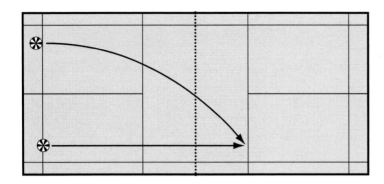

Fig 37 Flight path of an open face drop shot.

Fig 38 Racket and body position for a closed face drop shot.

Fig 39 Racket and body position for an open face drop shot. The similarity to the closed face drop shot can be deceptive.

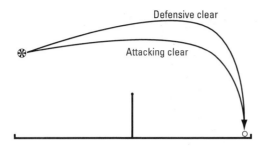

Fig 40 *Trajectory of a clear.*

Fig 41 *Racket and body preparation for a smash.*

Coaching Tips

- Position the body in line with and behind the shuttle.
- Point of contact to be in front of the player.
- Generate a full swing on to the shuttle to obtain maximum power.
- The body should move forward into the shot to aid recovery to the base.

Smash

The most explosive shot in all racket sports, the smash, when used correctly, can prove to be a most devastating weapon. As with the clear and drop shot, the smash has the same basic elements of preparation, execution and recovery. The difference with the smash is that it is hit with power and speed downward to the opponent's court.

Using good footwork, the player gets behind the shuttle so that it may be hit in front of him. The racket should be pointing up in preparation for the shot. As with the clear and the drop shot, the player's arm should be bent, ready to explode on to the shuttle. The wrist is then snapped down at point of impact giving the shuttle extra power and angle towards the opponent's court. As with all recovery movements, the player needs to keep his head up, back straight and

Fig 42 *Racket and body position at point of contact for a smash.*

Fig 43 Recovery position after a smash.

feet moving forward to maintain balance and control. The racket needs to be brought up as quickly as possible to be able to react to the next shot and should be carried in a central position.

Coaching Tips

- Get behind the shuttle.
- For power and downward angle, snap the wrist down as the racket hits the shuttle.
- Keep the back as straight as possible during the shot.
- Recover as quickly as possible with good movement and quick racket speed to the ready position.

Jump Smash

The jump smash is an advanced shot used by players to combine the smash with the explosive power of jumping up and moving forward. This type of smash may be used in all games.

The same basic techniques are used as for a normal smash. However, rather than stepping into the smash, the player jumps upward and sometimes forward to the shuttle. Jumping up at the shuttle has a number of results:

- the shuttle is intercepted earlier;
- the opponent has less time to prepare for a defensive reply;
- the higher the smash, the steeper the angle into the opposition's court;

Fig 44 Racket and body position at point of contact for a jump smash.

● the explosive movement of jumping forward and upward provide the hitter with increased power.

Net Shot

As the name suggests, this shot is played from around the net area back to the net area and can be played both on the forehand and backhand sides. The objective of a net shot is to force the opponent to hit a weak lift.

The net shot is played with an underarm movement, pushing the shuttle gently towards the net. The movement of the hitter is in the form of a lunge, with the racket arm and racket leg moving together towards the shuttle, keeping the racket high to ensure the shuttle is hit as early as possible.

The only real difference between playing on the forehand and backhand sides is that a backhand grip would be adopted when playing a net shot on the backhand side. Net shots can be played either straight or across court, which can increase the difficulty for the opposition with movement and the return shot.

Once the shot has been played, the hitter then recovers by pushing back towards the base position using both legs whilst ensuring that the racket does not drop, which is a common fault.

Coaching Tips
● Try to take shuttle as high as possible.
● Push through the shuttle, without lifting with arm or wrist.
● Lunge forward and push the shuttle at the same time.
● Do not allow the racket to drop.
● Recover with the racket up and in the ready position.
● Make sure the grip is correct.
● Hold the racket lightly with the grip position.

Net Kill

A net 'kill' is played when the opponent has played a loose shot over the net, providing an opportunity to attack the shuttle by hitting down from the net area. It can be played on both forehand and backhand sides.

The body movement is the same as the movement for a net shot, the only differences being:

● the racket head is held high (above the racket hand) to enable the player to take the shuttle above the net level;

*Fig 45 Racket
and body
position for a
forehand net
shot.*

*Fig 46 Racket
and body position
for a backhand
net shot.*

- the shuttle is tapped down from above net level with little or no racket arm movement as the hit comes from the player's wrist, and then the racket rebounds to ensure no follow through or risk of hitting the net (which is a fault whilst the shuttle is in play);
- the player sometimes has to move explosively into the net, so control and balance is very important. The movement required may be a step or jump.

Coaching Tips

- Move quickly up to the net.
- Reach forward to take the shuttle early.
- Do not swing the arm and racket at the shuttle.
- Use the wrist to create movement and power.
- Hold the handle of the racket higher up as this gives greater control.
- Allow the racket to rebound after the shot has been played.
- Do not hit the shuttle before it travels on to your side, it is a fault if played on the opponent's side.
- The foot position on the lunge leg should be forward, not sideways.

Fig 47 Racket and body position for a forehand net kill.

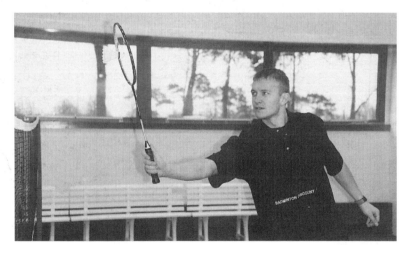

Fig 48 Racket and body position for a backhand net kill.

28

Lift

The main objective of this shot is to play the shuttle from in front of the body from the forecourt area and attempt to 'lift' it above the opponent's head and racket. This shot can be played on both backhand and forehand sides.

The lift is played with an underarm movement and from a lunge position. The movement should be made to look exactly the same as the movement in the net shot. If this is done correctly, the opposition will have great difficulty in judging which shot is being played until the last moment. The hitter moves forward to play the shot, which will look like a net shot. However, just before striking the shuttle, the hand and the wrist unlock, powerfully lifting and sending the shuttle into the opposition's rear tramlines.

The racket head at the point of impact is lifted through the shuttle with the use of the wrist and elbow. The recovery for the lift is the same as for the net shot with both legs pushing back towards a good base position and the racket returning to the ready position. The forehand and backhand lifts are played in a similar fashion but it is important to use the correct grips.

Coaching Tips
● Try to take the shuttle as high as possible at the net.
● Do not allow the racket to drop too low.
● Recover with the racket up and in the ready position.
● Use the wrist to lift through the shuttle.
● Finish with a full racket swing upward.

Fig 49 Racket and body position for a forehand lift.

Fig 50 Racket and body position for a backhand lift.

CHAPTER 4
Backhand Shots

The backhand shot is looked upon by most beginners as the most difficult shot to produce from the rear court. One of the main reasons for this is because it is not a natural swing. However, once the basic techniques have been mastered, most players find that backhand is not only simple to play but also only requires a small amount of effort. Technique and timing are much more important than strength in mastering this shot.

Not all backhand shots are played with the basic backhand grip (*see* Chapter 1). The grip should be adjusted depending on the type of shot being played and whether the shuttle is in front or behind the body at the time. The basic backhand grip is used for backhand serves or net shots. The universal backhand grip is used for shots such as backhand clears, drops and pushes.

The three elements of preparation, execution and recovery mentioned for forehand shots apply equally to backhand shots.

Clear

Having made sure that the suitable backhand

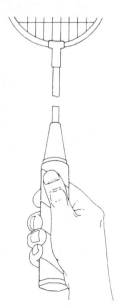

Fig 51 Backhand grip.

Fig 52 Universal backhand grip.

grip has been adopted in preparation for the shot, the player's racket should be following the flight path of the shuttle – this will adjust the body into the correct position. The player's footwork should position the body underneath the falling shuttle with the elbow close in beside the body and the racket arm bent for a back swing in preparation for the forward swing to commence.

Fig 53 Backhand footwork movement.

Fig 54 Moving into the correct position for a rear court shot.

The player then, at the correct moment, extends his arm and swings the racket up to meet the shuttle, making contact at the earliest possible point. The wrist is used to flick powerfully at the shuttle and then stops to ensure that no follow through takes place, which allows full power to be transferred to the shuttle. The racket is then moved back into the recovery position ready for the next shot, with the feet moving back towards the base.

Fig 55 Racket and body preparation for a backhand shot from rear court.

BELOW LEFT: Fig 56 Moving into the correct position.

BELOW: Fig 57 Arm and racket in the correct position.

Fig 58 Racket and body position at point of contact with the shuttle.

Fig 59 Recovery position after the shot has been played.

Coaching Tips

- Follow the flight of shuttle with the racket in preparation for the shot.
- Keep the racket arm and elbow close into the body.
- Hit the shuttle at a high point of impact; do not allow the shuttle to drop too low.

- The wrist should be flicked powerfully towards the shuttle.
- Do not allow the racket to follow through.
- Land the racket leg at the same time as contact with the shuttle to make a solid base impact position.

Fig 60 Racket angle when hitting a backhand drop shot.

Drop Shot

This shot should be a carbon copy of the backhand clear with only the following exceptions:

- the wrist is not used to powerfully flick towards the shuttle;
- the total arm movement is not as powerful;
- the racket angle at point of contact with the shuttle is directed towards the net to create a good downward angle for the shuttle.

As with the backhand clear, it is important not to allow the racket to follow through downwards immediately after the shot has been played as this will tend to drag the shuttle into the net, although a short follow through may be useful.

Coaching Tips
<ul><li>Hit the shuttle with a high point of impact and do not allow the shuttle to drop too low.</li><li>The wrist should be held in a firm position, but not solid, to enable the correct angle to be created to hit the drop shot to the fore-court of the opponent's court.</li><li>As with all backhand shots, it helps with timing if the racket leg lands at the same time as the hit.</li></ul>

Smash

The backhand smash is an advanced shot and should only be played when the player is in a position to recover quickly. The movement to the shuttle is the same as for the backhand clear and backhand drop shot.

There should be no or very little follow through as all the power of arm and wrist is transferred to the shuttle with an abrupt halt of the movement. The player's wrist should be angled diagonally downward to create the correct flight path for the shuttle.

As with all power shots, the harder the shuttle is hit, the less the control on the shuttle. Therefore it it important not to over hit with this shot.

Fig 61 Racket angle when hitting a backhand smash.

Coaching Tips

- Move quickly to get into position early.
- High elbow position at point of impact.
- Strong wrist action to flick down at the shuttle.
- Do not follow through with the racket after the hit.
- Recover quickly back towards the net.

CHAPTER 5

Match Play

Once the basic shots have been mastered, it is then possible to play a game. There are differences between the court areas for doubles and singles. In a singles game, the side tramlines are out of court: in doubles, the whole court is 'in' during a rally. It is important to know the court area for both of these games when serving. (*See* figures 64–65.)

SINGLES

Ladies singles are played up to 11 points a game in the best of three games. Men's singles are played up to 15 points a game in the best of three games.

Setting

When playing a game of ladies singles, if the score gets to 10–10, the player who got to 10 first has the choice of either:

- playing to 11 points (play straight through); or
- playing to 13 points (play setting).

When playing a game of men's singles, if the score gets to 14–14, the player who got to 14 first has the choice of either:

- playing to 15 points (play straight through); or
- playing to 17 points (play setting).

When playing men's, ladies or mixed doubles, the same rules for setting apply as for the men's singles.

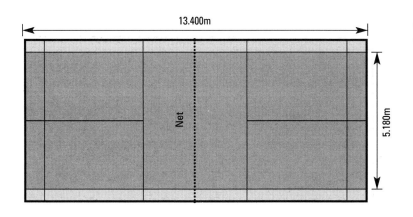

Fig 62 The singles court.

Fig 63 The doubles court.

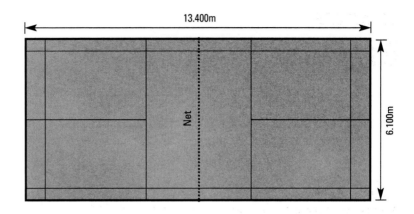

Fig 64 Singles court serving area.

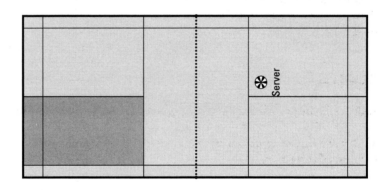

Fig 65 Doubles court serving area.

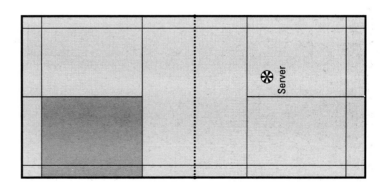

Fig 66 Camilla Martin of Denmark at full stretch retrieving a difficult backhand. Photo: Peter Richardson.

Playing the Game

Players should 'toss' to see who starts the match or has choice of ends and then the match starts with the serve from the right-hand side of the court. A high serve is normally used in singles to send the opponent to the back of the court, as this gives the server time to prepare for the return. However, if the opponent has a strong and accurate smash then a low serve to the forecourt could be used, thus stopping the opponent from smashing. The use of the low serve is becoming more prevalent in elite level singles. Once the server has served then a base position should be adopted, which enables the receiver to cover the return from a central position.

The base position is not an exact place on the court. It is the place that a player should try to return to after playing the shot. A player should always attempt to be in a well-balanced position when the opponent hits the shuttle: from that position he can perform his push start to move towards the next shot.

The shaded areas in the following illustrations show the ideal base position relative to where the shuttle is being hit from by a player's opponent. These areas would give the receiver the best opportunity to cover their court. However, the player may find that there is not sufficient time to recover to these positions.

Fig 67 Shaded area shows central base for singles.

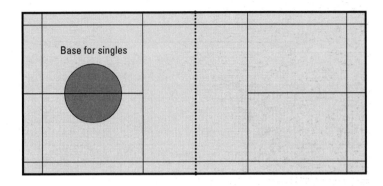

Fig 68 Base area for covering a shot from the forehand rear court.

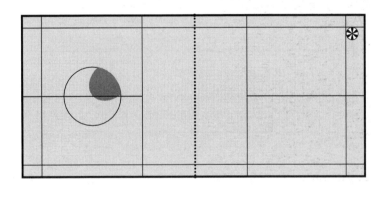

Fig 69 Base area for covering a shot from the backhand rear court.

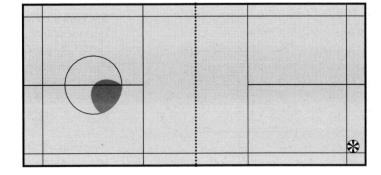

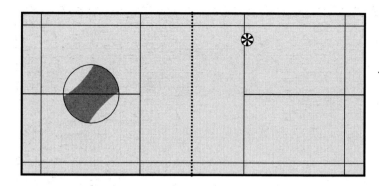

Fig 70 Base area for covering a shot from the forehand forecourt.

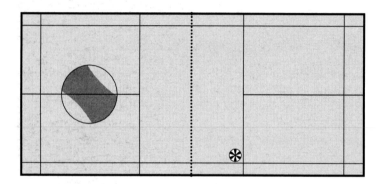

Fig 71 Base area for covering a shot from the backhand forecourt.

When working out a base position it is also important to be aware of the flight time of the shot that has just played. For example, it is unrealistic to say that if a player hits a smash to the opposing mid-court area, he will be able to recover to a forward base position: the player will only be able to reach a deep central position.

Coaching Tips

- Use the whole of the court to exploit the opponent's weaknesses.
- Rallies in singles are generally more physically demanding, so fitness is essential.
- Vary attacking shots around the court. Try not to become predictable.

Singles is a very demanding game and it is important to be able to play a full range of shots. A high level of physical fitness, 100 per cent concentration throughout, and self-motivation are paramount, which makes it an extremely tough game to play.

LEVEL DOUBLES

Scoring

The same rules apply for setting as for the men's singles. At the start of a match, only one player from the serving team is allowed to serve. He continues until they lose a rally, thereby giving the service to the opposition. The next player to serve is from the opposing pair and serves from his right-hand service

Fig 72 Peter Gade Christensen of Denmark demononstrating the explosive movement of a jump smash. Photo: Peter Richardson.

box. He also continues to serve from alternating service boxes until his pair lose, then his partner serves. When both players have lost their serve, it passes back to the first pair. This pattern continues throughout the whole of the game. Each time a pair serves and wins the rally they score a point, and so on, until they finish the game.

Positioning

Fig 73 shows the correct positions for all players at the beginning of a game of level doubles. Both pairs are in an attacking position – one player at the front and one behind. Ideally, the server tries to keep the attack by playing a good, low serve which forces the receiver to play the shuttle either back to the net, which the server can then intercept and attack, or force a lift up to the rear court where the server's partner can then attack by hitting down.

When playing level doubles, it is vitally important that the players know where to

41

Fig 73 Players' positions for the start of a level doubles.

stand for attack and defence. When players attack in doubles, the typical positions are one at the front of the court and one at the back. If the shuttle is lifted to the back, an attacking shot can be played either as an attempted winner or to create a weak return that can be killed by the player at the net. It is important that, when attacking, the player at the front is positioned behind the 'T' in the forecourt, as this gives him time to see the shuttle and position himself for the kill.

Fig 74 Central defence position.

Fig 75 Defence position from right-hand side attack.

Fig 76 Defence position from left-hand side attack.

Fig 77 Attack position for central attack.

Fig 78 Attack position for right-hand side.

Fig 79 Attack position for left-hand side.

Defending in Doubles

The strength of any match-winning doubles team is the ability to defend well and then turn defence into attack. A defending pair should use block shots, pushes and net shots to achieve this, but it is important to use these shots at the right time and to call to each other whilst defending to avoid racket clashes.

If a player has to play a lift in doubles, it is important that it is deep into the opposition's court – this makes defending easier for pairs.

When defending, players stand side by side, which allows them to cover the width of the court. Each player also covers the front and back of the half-court he is standing in.

Fig 80 Lee Dong-Soo and Yoo Yong-Sung (near side) of Korea showing good attacking positions for men's doubles. Photo: Peter Richardson.

Fig 81 Good defensive positions.

Coaching Tips

The easiest way to remember where you should be during a rally is:

- If your side can hit the shuttle down – attack front and back positions;
- If your side has lifted the shuttle – defend with side positions.

A good tactic to adopt for most games is to try and make the opponents lift the shuttle, which will allow an attack by hitting downward.

Attacking in Doubles

During rallies, it is crucial for pairs to try to gain the attack at the earliest opportunity and maintain it. The net player's role is to try to intercept shots as well as killing any weak net returns by the opponents. The rear court player's role is to hit with attacking shots such as smashes and drops, trying to create weak returns that may provide an opportunity to attack. A good attacking tactic in doubles is to smash down towards the opponent's body, as this may result in a weak reply.

MIXED DOUBLES

Mixed doubles is probably the hardest game to play. It is difficult to remember where to be and who is to play which shot during the course of a rally. At top level play, the man generally controls the rear of the court and

Fig 82 Movement to the shuttle as demonstrated by Chung Jae-Hee (left) and Ra Kyung-Min (right) of Korea is an essential part of doubles defence. Photo: Peter Richardson.

> ### Coaching Tips
>
> - When standing in the forecourt, players should always have the racket up and ready in front of the body. This is an attacking position.
> - When defending, players should adopt the position illustrated (Fig 81).
> - Always call to your partner and never afraid to shout 'yours' or 'mine'.
> - Stand in a ready position with legs bent and body weight on the balls of the feet as often as possible.
> - Remember when playing doubles that it is a team game and you are working with your partner, so always look to cover him and he will cover for you.
> - Be patient when playing, resist going for a winning shot too soon. The pair who makes fewest mistakes generally wins.
> - Try not to hit and watch only.

the woman controls the forecourt area, but there is no rule about this. If a woman is as strong or stronger than her partner, a level doubles strategy can be adopted. It is important that both players understand each other's role at the outset, otherwise this may lead to a dispute during the match itself.

Positioning for the Service

Women
A woman may use the same serving position as for level doubles. However, when the man is serving, the woman's position changes. The woman places herself in front of the man, to the right of the central 'T'position if the man is left-handed, and to the left of the central 'T' position if the man is right-handed. This positioning will help the woman control the front of the court and allows the man to cover the rear court.

Men
To serve, the man should position himself a

Fig 83 Start of a mixed doubles match.

Fig 84 Liu Yong of China demonstrates his explosive power from the back of the court for mixed doubles. Photo: Peter Richardson.

Fig 85 Service from left-hand side.

Fig 86 Service from right-hand side.

couple of steps back from his normal serving position as he only needs to be able to cover the rear court – the forecourt area is covered by his partner, who stands in front of him during the serve.

Coaching Tip

When returning a low serve in doubles, it is important to attempt to attack whenever possible. This can be done by playing net shots or pushes, but it is important not to play the same shots over and over again – keep your opponents guessing.

Tactics during the Rally

A very simple way to describe the tactics in mixed doubles is that the man should try to play straight shots whenever possible, and the woman should aim to adopt a cross-court position during the rally.

During the rally, it is important that the woman tries to dominate the net area, to be aggressive and not back away towards the rear court. Whenever smashing, it is always good for the man to smash with a straight, steep downward angle, as this will make the net kills for the woman easier from a block return.

When the woman is defending the cross-court smash, her racket should be up in a ready position and at face level, with her body turned towards the direction from which the smash is being hit. The position on the court is also important because if she is too close to the net, the reaction time to the smash is reduced. If she is too far back, the return would have to be lifted, allowing attacking opportunities to the opposition. She should be a short distance behind the service line, taking care when hitting the return not to allow the opposition further attacking opportunities.

There are no hard and fast rules when playing mixed doubles: the tactics adopted will depend on individual strengths and weaknesses. When played correctly, mixed doubles is the most enjoyable game to watch.

Fig 87 Mixed doubles defence positions.

Coaching Tips

- The woman should not to attempt to play shots that are either just out of reach or just behind her body.
- If a lift or clear has to be played, the woman should try to play across court and the man should try to play straight, so that both players are positioned correctly for the return.

SUMMARY

When playing in matches or tournaments, an important part of any player's preparation is to watch the opponent to try and assess his strengths and weaknesses.

A player should also consult his coach, if he has one, about the tactics he could adopt during a match. This must be done before going on court, as a player is not allowed coaching until the interval between games, and this can sometimes be too late to change to a new game plan.

During matches it is vitally important that communication between players is maintained. This can take the form of either verbal or physical encouragement. It is equally important that, if a team's tactics are not working, no time is lost in trying something different.

CHAPTER 6

Advanced Shots and Routines

DECEPTIVE AND CREATIVE SHOTS

Performed correctly, a deceptive or a creative shot should make the opponent late getting into position to hit the shuttle, or unable to reach it at all.

A deceptive shot is:

- a shot that makes the opponent anticipate wrongly, sending him in the wrong direction;
- a shot that makes the opponent pause and wait to move until you hit the shuttle;
- when a player hits the shuttle fractionally earlier or later than expected in a different direction.

Deception can be created by body movements, changes in racket head direction, or merely not doing the obvious.

A creative shot is:

- a shot that develops an opening in a pattern of play;
- not a winning shot, but one which may lead to a point-winning situation;
- a shot taken at the earliest opportunity to decrease the length of time the opponent has to play his shot.

> **Coaching Tips**
>
> - All shots depend on speed, trajectory and whether the player jumps when hitting the shuttle.
> - The quality of creativity and deception is dependant on shot preparation.
> - Creative shots do not have to be deceptive.
> - All deceptive shots are designed to be creative.

The following shots are for players who have a clear and precise knowledge of advanced badminton shots and are technically aware of how slices, cuts and brush shots are played.

DECEPTIVE SHOTS FROM THE REAR COURT

Forehand Check/Stop Smash

This shot is normally played straight. The aim of the shot is to convince the opponent that a smash or clear is about to be played. The opponent's body position will be such that he will be waiting for a deep shot and it will be extremely difficult for him to move forward quickly and cover a deceptive drop shot. This shot is seen most frequently in doubles and is used to set up a greater attacking opportunity.

Forehand Punch Clear

This shot is normally played straight or cross-court. The aim of the shot is to convince the opponent that a smash or drop shot is about to be played, and to catch him moving forward.

Backhand Reverse Slice Drop

This shot is played straight. The aim is to wrongfoot the opponent by brushing across the shuttle sending him the wrong way – an extremely difficult shot to play.

Backhand Punch Clear

This shot is normally played straight. The aim is to hit a flat backhand clear quickly past the opponent, making him think that the shot being played is actually a drop shot and catching him moving in towards the net.

DECEPTIVE SHOTS FROM THE FORECOURT

Forehand and Backhand Swipe Shots

This shot is normally played either straight or cross-court. The main aim is to hit the shuttle flat down the line or cross-court in order to wrong foot the opponent by delaying the shot until he has committed to a direction.

Double Swing Shot

This shot is normally played with a delay action from the net area. The aim is to deceive the opponent by first playing a dummy swing, immediately followed by the actual hit. This requires an extremely rapid

racket head movement and a high level of control.

Backhand Low Cross-Court Net Shot

This shot is played from the net area. The aim is to delay the hitting action until the opponent has stared to move and committed himself.

Net Shot Played with a Big Swing

This shot is played from the net area. The aim is to delay the hit until the opponent has anticipated a lift to the rear court by making a large swing action at the shuttle but hitting it with a glancing blow.

Lifting from a Small/Short Swing

This shot is played from the net area. The aim is to fake a net shot, making the opponent move to the forecourt then hit to the rear court. This shot requires a rapid racket movement, and the player to be highly alert.

CREATIVE SHOTS FROM THE REAR COURT

Forehand Slice Drop Shot

This shot is normally played straight or cross-court. The aim of the shot is to force the opponent to react quickly and suddenly, thus manoeuvering him out of position. The shot is played with a fast racket swing and accuracy. The shot can be played as a winner but is used mainly as a creative shot to create a winning opportunity

Forehand Reverse Slice Drop Shot

This shot is normally played straight or cross-court. The aim is to wrongfoot the opponent. The hitter's wrist is turned across the shuttle, brushing in a different direction. The opponent will be focusing on the arm action, not the wrist. The shot can be played as a winner but is used mainly as a creative shot to create a winning opportunity.

Forehand Smash

This shot is played straight or cross-court. The aim is to create either a winning shot or a weak reply.

Forehand Stick Smash

This shot is played straight or cross-court. The aim is to create a weak return from the opponent by playing a very steep, angled smash with accuracy.

Flat Clear

This shot is played straight or cross-court. The aim is to obtain a weak reply. The clear is hit flat with speed, just over the head of the opponent.

Backhand Slice Drop Shot

This shot is played cross-court. The aim is to catch the opponent out as the racket head speed is very fast.

Backhand Smash

This shot is played straight or cross-court. The aim is to create a winning opportunity by playing the shot, which is often unexpected.

Backhand Cross-Court Clear

The aim of this shot is to wrongfoot the opponent by catching him out of position, and by making him think that an alternative shot is being played. The hitter should be aware that a quick recovery is essential to cover any straight reply.

Backhand Clip

This shot is played straight. The aim is to play a fast drop with little movement, which gives the opposition very little choice in returns and little time to respond.

CREATIVE SHOTS FROM THE FORECOURT

Net Shot

This shot can be played with spin or tumble, straight or cross-court. The aim is to force a net reply or a weak lift as the spin or tumble on the shuttle will not give the opponent clean contact.

Flat Fast Lift

This shot can be played on both forehand and backhand sides. The aim is to reduce the time available to an opponent to position himself correctly and play an effective shot in response.

Coaching Tips

- The shuttle must be taken as high as possible.
- The shuttle must be taken as early as possible.
- The receiver's racket must be positioned in front of the body and in a high position.
- The correct grip must be used when playing the various shots.

Flat Push

This shot can be played straight or cross-court. The aim is to make the opponent think that a deep lift is being played by pushing the shuttle to a mid-court position.

CREATIVE AND DECEPTIVE SHOTS FROM THE RETURN OF THE LOW SERVE

Backhand Double Fake

This shot is played on the even side. The aim is to send the opponent the wrong way because he has followed the first swing action. This requires a very rapid arm action and a high level of control.

Forehand Cut Return

This shot is played from the odd side. The aim is to take the shuttle early with a very rapid racket head swing, the shuttle actually going straight.

Forehand and Backhand Brush Returns

This shot is played to the centre of the court from both sides. The aim is to brush across the shuttle with the racket face and send the shuttle down the centre of the court. The rear court player follows the path of the racket and then moves to the side. As this is no more than a glancing blow to the shuttle, it does not fly far.

Forehand Reverse Return

This shot is played cross-court from the odd side. The aim is to make the opponent think the shuttle is travelling to the rear court, but it actually travels to the forecourt. Excellent racket control is required for this shot.

MOVEMENT ROUTINES

The purpose of movement routines is for a player to rehearse and practise movement all around the court. The following routines are designed to enable a player to master correct footwork and movement techniques.

With all movement around the court, it is not only the footwork that should be efficient – the racket carriage is also important. A player moves with his body and racket to the shuttle. In many cases the racket moves first and then the body: this helps with taking the shuttle early and movement efficiency.

All the shots described here are suitable for players who have grasped the basics of stroke play and who now wish to expand their repertoire of shots and develop their game.

When working on shots and movement from all areas of the court, it is essential that both the feeder and the worker observe the following points:

- the feeder has to be accurate and controlled when hitting shots;
- the feeder must bear in mind that they are practising their skills;
- the hitter will only get out of the practice what he puts in;
- the work rate will drop below an effective level if the hitter is overworked.

There are numerous ways of developing shots and movements into game situations. The following routines should prove useful.

Shot Restrictions

Playing games with shot restrictions are always a tremendous way of making a player think whilst playing a game by hitting alternative shots.

Fig 88 shows the singles court with only the forecourt and rear court (shaded areas)

Fig 88 Rear court, forecourt game.

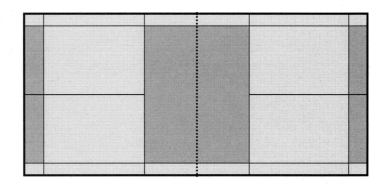

Fig 89 Half-court singles game.

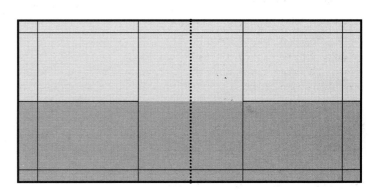

Fig 90 Two versus one.

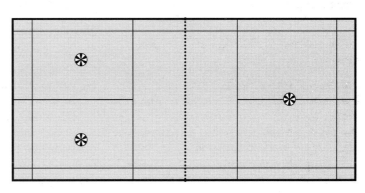

being 'in'. The practice would help players hit to a deep rear court area and improve play in the area of the net.

Half-court singles (Fig 89) is designed for players to practise movement and rally-building. The ability to play a wide range of shots and fitness are essential for this.

For a pressured singles (Fig 90), a game of 2v1 can be played on court. This is played on a singles court and is great for fitness, foot-work, speed around the court, and shot selection.

Three-Corner Routines

The three-corner shot routine (Fig 91) is a

55

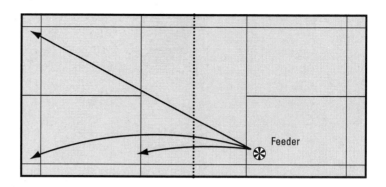

Fig 91 Three-corner routine.

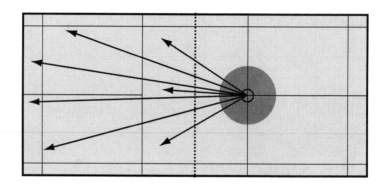

Fig 92 Playing to the centre.

game where the feeder chooses any three corners to play into in a random pattern. The hitter has to return the shuttle to the feeder every time. The feeder can also move around the court after a number of rallies to make the hitter alternate his return. This is an extremely strenuous routine, so change the hitter after three minutes of work.

Playing to the centre of the court is another routine that is designed for the hitter to return all shots to the centre of the feeder's court, who returns the shuttle all round the hitter's court. The feeder can play slower or faster shots to change the pace. The focus of this routine is to play safer shots, which is will build consistency into a player's game, and reduce his rate of error. It will also improve a player's fitness level, as the rallies will last longer during the routines.

Net Kill Routines

The feeder throws the shuttle to one side and then the other, allowing the hitter time to recover to a mid-forecourt position (Fig 93).

The hitter plays the first net kill and then recovers, focusing on the racket position and body posture, in anticipation of the next shuttle. The feeder can alternate the feed, making the hitter work harder as he cannot guess where the shuttle will be played next.

Defensive Routines

This routine is played by a feeder throwing a number of shuttles down towards the left- and right-hand sides of the hitter's court, simulating fast and slow drop shots (Fig 94). The hitter returns to a central base position

Fig 93 Net kill routine.

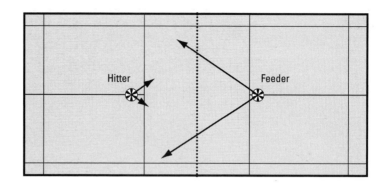

Fig 94 Defence routine.

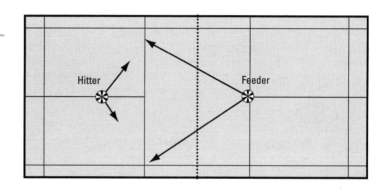

after every shot. The shots played by the hitter can be a mixture of net shots, pushes and flat lifts. In this exercise, the hitter should be working on both his shots and his movement – the feeder should allow time for recovery. This is a multi-feed routine where the hitter should be hitting twelve to sixteen shuttles per feed.

Rally-Building Routines

The feeder stands in one position and the hitter has to return the shuttle for the first five shots of the rally (the rally is only to be played on half-court). After the fifth shot has been played by the hitter, the feeder shouts 'live'. A normal rally can then commence where the shuttle can be played anywhere within the half-court by both players and the point is won or lost as in a normal game. The routine can be played as a mini-match up to five points and then can be swapped over. The purpose of this practice is to build consistency into a player's game by not making unforced errors early in a rally.

DOUBLES ROUTINES

These routines are designed for pairs playing together during practice, as doubles is all about teamship.

An excellent exercise is for one pair to play defensively and the other to attack. Alternatively, during practice the emphasis can be on turning defense into attack, and not lifting too often by blocking and moving into an attack position.

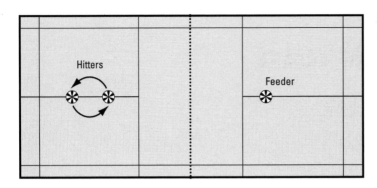

Fig 95 Rotational work on court.

All good doubles pairs have the ability to both defend well and move into attacking positions. The routines should be based around this – an awareness of movement is the key to success.

Rotational Movement

This type of routine can be played from different positions in the mid-court and fore-court. The shots from the hitters can be played soft or hard, and can be directed to different parts of the court.

The feeder can dictate the pace at which the hitters rotate around each other: this then simulates the varying pace of matches. This type of routine also makes the hitters aware that they must move continuously during a rally, which will enable them to move efficiently towards their next shot.

Shadow Play

Shadow play is a good way in which to practise movement around the court. By practising the correct movement and technique without actually hitting a shuttle, it is possible to focus on the movement to and from the shot without having to worry about the shuttle being in or out. This can be done for all movement practices around the court. When practising shadow badminton, a player should try to picture the shuttle flight, contact point and shot that is being played.

Coaching Tip

Skipping is one of the best ways to improve footwork and is a great way to work on becoming quick and light with footwork movement. Skipping to music is an excellent way of practice and alleviates boredom. It is important that skipping is done on the correct floor surface, ideally a sprung floor, not concrete, as this can lead to leg injuries.

SUMMARY

All movement practices should be done with total control and court awareness – without racket and body control it would be extremely difficult to control the shuttle.

CHAPTER 7

Footwork and Movement

A successful badminton player needs to have excellent footwork and movement skills to enable him to cover the court efficiently and with control. These skills not only help a player to get to the shuttle quickly, but also to control the shuttle when playing shots, and to recover quickly after the shot has been played.

PUSH START

Movement on court begins with the push start. This is where the player pushes downward to enable the muscles to flex and react to the direction required to play a shot. The push start movement is used just as an opponent strikes the shuttle. This is very important as it enables the player to react efficiently to the shuttle. The push start is the basis of all movement around the badminton court – without it, the player would find it difficult to react to shots.

MOVEMENT TO MID-COURT

Base position to push start. The player should transfer his body weight on to the right leg to move to the left or on to the left leg to move right. The player's head should remain

steady and upright as this will maintain upper body balance throughout the shot, including the recovery. In preparation for the next shot, a chase movement should be adopted for the recovery of the body whilst keeping the racket in front and central.

Fig 96 Push start position with flexed legs.

Fig 97 Forehand preparation for mid-court shot.

Fig 98 Forehand hit for mid-court shot.

Fig 99 Forehand recovery after mid-court shot.

Fig 100 Backhand preparation for mid-court shot.

Fig 101 Backhand hit for mid-court shot.

Fig 102 Backhand recovery after mid-court shot.

FORECOURT MOVEMENT – FOREHAND AND BACKHAND

Base position to push start. The player then moves in the direction required by pushing off either one or both legs. As the player is moving forward, the legs should be positioned so that the racket leg is the lead leg: this will enable a lunge position to be adopted.

The timing of the shot will be improved if the landing of the racket leg and shot is simultaneous. The landing of the player's front lunging leg should be held heel-to-toe, as this will help control, balance and recovery. Both legs should then be used to push into a recovery position and chase backward to a base position to prepare for the next shot.

Racket position as seen in the photographs is in front and controlled in preparation for the next shot.

Fig 104 Forehand hit for forecourt shot.

Fig 103 Forehand preparation for forecourt shot.

Fig 105 Forehand recovery after forecourt shot.

Fig 106 Backhand preparation for forecourt shot.

Fig 107 Backhand hit for forecourt shot.

Fig 108 Backhand recovery after forecourt shot.

Fig 109 Forehand preparation for rear court shot.

REAR COURT MOVEMENT – FOREHAND

Base position to push start. Turn the body so that the racket arm is moving towards the forehand rear court – turned hips will enable the player to chase backwards. The player's racket arm lifts into the preparation position, at shoulder height, ready to hit the shot. The shot is then played with a high reach and both feet walking forward through the shot. A straight body position should be maintained throughout the shot. This should be followed by chase movements towards the base in preparation for the next shot.

REAR COURT MOVEMENT – BACKHAND

Base position to push start. Keep legs apart and pivot on the non-racket leg to allow the body to turn towards the backhand corner. The non-racket shoulder should lead the movement, and the player should have his racket arm up, pointing in the direction of the shuttle. The player should then strike the shuttle at the earliest opportunity and stop as soon as possible after point of contact. At the same time as contact, the racket leg should make contact with the ground to help timing, balance, control and recovery. Once the shot

Fig 110 Forehand hit for rear court shot.

Fig 111 Forecourt recovery after rear court shot.

*Fig 112
Backhand
preparation for
rear court shot.*

Fig 113 Backhand hit for rear court shot.

Fig 114 Backhand recovery after rear court shot.

has been played, the player pushes off the racket leg to enable the body to rotate back towards the net and base position, chase back ready for the next shot.

CHAPTER 8

Nutrition

'Training diets have to achieve and maintain an appropriate body mass and level of body fat, and, have to promote optimal return from training by providing a nutritional environment that allows for recovery between training sessions.'[1]

The link between nutrition and performance has been widely accepted, and nutrition now plays a very important role within the training programme of many athletes. The fact that good nutrition influences not only performance, but also long-term health is generally undisputed, but in order to maximize such benefits, dietary needs must be looked at on an individual basis. Although the principles behind dietary intake are similar for all athletes, dietary advice will vary according to sex, age, body composition, lifestyle and type and intensity of exercise. The individual's training programme must, of course, also be taken into consideration.

The key element in an effective and efficient dietary plan is balance. Active players need to combine high levels of carbohydrate (55–65 per cent), average levels of protein (10–25 per cent) and low levels of fat (15–20 per cent) along with a low sugar and salt intake. As well as this, to avoid deficiencies within the body, the diet must provide high levels of vitamins and minerals.

With the onset of regular training, the body's nutritional needs increase because of the rise in energy consumption which, in turn, alters the metabolism of carbohydrate, fat and protein which ultimately affects the body's composition. Balanced nutrition is therefore of the utmost importance both to success in sport and improving general health.

To get the most out of a badminton training programme and to accentuate overall performance, the correct nutrients need to be consumed. This will increase energy levels, delay fatigue, enable the player to train harder for longer and recover more rapidly.

As training intensity increases, the ratio of carbohydrate to fat intake changes. The higher the training intensity, the greater the proportion of carbohydrate used, and the lower the proportion of fat. For example, when running at 9.5km/h (6mph), approximately 60 per cent of the fuel mixture comes from carbohydrate and 40 per cent from fat; when walking at 6.5km/h (4mph), only 40 per cent of the fuel mixture comes from carbohydrate and 60 per cent from fat.

As the duration of aerobic training increases, the contribution from carbohydrate decreases due to the continuous depletion of stores from prolonged bouts of exercise, and, as stores deplete, the total fuel mixture must depend less on the contribution made by carbohydrate and more on the contribution that comes from fat.

When planning a diet, it is important to consider the type, the amount and the timing of carbohydrate intake. Exercising with low levels or sub-optimal carbohydrate stores, leads to:

- below par performance;
- early onset of fatigue;
- slower recovery;
- decreased training intensity;
- decreased training gains;
- greater risk of injury;
- 'burn out' or overtraining syndrome (if chronic).

The Best Sources of Carbohydrate

The two main aspects to consider when identifying the best sources of carbohydrate are the nutritional quality provided by the carbohydrate source, and the rate at which the carbohydrate is absorbed into the bloodstream

From a nutritional point of view, the best choices are those foods that contain naturally occurring sources of sugars, such as fruit, vegetables and milk, and those that combine complex carbohydrates, such as pasta and grains. This is because these foods also contain other important nutrients such as vitamins, minerals, protein and fibre. On the other hand, from a performance point of view, the best choice of carbohydrate depends primarily upon the timing of intake in relation to the workout.

All carbohydrates are broken down into simple sugars and transported in the bloodstream as glucose and are equally capable of being used by the muscle cells and made into glycogen. Consequently, as far as glycogen manufacture is concerned, the type of carbohydrate consumed is irrelevant.

However, the speed at which the carbohydrate is converted into blood glucose and transported to the muscles is important. The glycaemic index (GI) in foods indicates the rise in blood glucose levels: the faster and higher the blood glucose rises, the higher the GI. For example, consumption of high GI carbohydrates are advantageous during the first two hours after exercise or towards the end of a long, hard workout, when glycogen stores are low. Studies have shown that consuming approximately 1g of carbohydrate per kg of body weight within the two-hour post-exercise period speeds up glycogen refuelling and therefore the recovery time. This type of carbohydrate proves most beneficial prior to or in-between workouts, as the body absorbs it more slowly over a longer period of time.

In contrast to these findings, there are times when it is beneficial to consume lower GI carbohydrates. This may be achieved by selecting foods with a range of GI levels and combining them with proteins and fats. For example, combine rice (high GI) with beans (low GI); baked potato (high GI) with tuna (protein); or bread (high GI) with cheese (protein and fat).

Athletes should obtain at least 60 per cent of their energy requirements from carbohydrates, which amounts to a daily intake of 450g (15¾oz) for a person consuming 3,000 calories a day. Depending on the frequency and intensity of training, most athletes will require 5–10g (⅕–⅖oz) of carbohydrate per kilogram of body weight. In more realistic food terms, 450g (15¾oz) of carbohydrate is found in thirty bananas, twelve large potatoes or ten chocolate bars.

Examples of portions of food containing approximately 50g (1¾oz) of carbohydrate include:

- 3 slices bread or toast;
- banana sandwich;
- average-size baked potato with 113g (4oz) of baked beans;
- 57g (2oz) breakfast cereal with ½ pint of low-fat milk;

- 2–3 bananas;
- 1 pint isotonic drink;
- 2–3 pieces dried fruit or small cereal bars;
- 7 rice cakes;
- 200g (7oz) cooked pasta;
- 170g (6oz) cooked rice.

High-Carbohydrate Diets

In endurance events, elevated glycogen stores help suppress the onset of fatigue and dehydration. Although this is beneficial, it may also cause muscle stiffness and discomfort during exercise. Along with this, the extra body weight is likely to be detrimental, especially in events such as doubles in badminton, where speed, agility and flexibility are more important than endurance. The following is an example of a high-carbohydrate diet.

Breakfast
250ml fruit juice
2tbs dried fruit
6 Weetabix
300ml skimmed milk
2 slices toast
2tsp jam

Mid-Morning Break
honey and banana sandwich
250ml fruit juice

Lunch
3 cups cooked rice, topped with a vegetable sauce
2 pieces fruit
250ml fruit juice

Afternoon Tea
2 slices raisin toast
2tsp jam
1 piece fruit
250ml fruit juice

Dinner
small serving lean red meat, poultry or fish
3 cups cooked pasta
2–3 vegetables
2 slices bread
2 pieces fruit or a medium fruit salad
250ml fruit juice

Supper
honey and sultana sandwich
250ml fruit juice

Dietary Analysis
Energy	16,800kj (4,000kcal)
Protein	15 per cent of total energy
Fat	5 per cent of total energy
Carbohydrate	80 per cent of total energy

PRE-COMPETITION MEALS

Six Hours Pre-Event

There are three nutrition targets:

- to increase carbohydrate fuel stores and ensure any undesirable effects of energy utilization are avoided;
- to ensure adequate hydration;
- to provide a comfortable gastrointestinal state, avoiding any GI problems that may reduce exercise performance and cause hunger due to a long period without eating.

One Hour Pre-Event

These foods need to have a high loading of carbohydrates that are easily digested. Proposed food consumption strategies should be tested during training to be certain that they do not cause any unwelcome side-effects. Minimal levels of fat are recommended as it delays the digestive process and does not contribute to liver glycogen stores effectively. To ensure optimal hydration, excessive protein intake should be avoided as it increases water excretion. Examples of pre-event meals include:

- breakfast cereal, skimmed milk, fresh or canned fruit;
- muffins or crumpets with jam or honey;
- pancakes with syrup;
- toast with baked beans;
- baked potatoes with low-fat filling;
- creamed rice made with skimmed milk;
- spaghetti with tomato or low-fat sauce;
- rolls or sandwiches with banana filling;
- fruit salad with low-fat yoghurt.[2]

EATING BETWEEN MATCHES AND AFTER EVENTS

Sports that consist of a series of heats or rounds such as badminton often cause problems to players in terms of maintaining adequate supplies of energy and fluids. While abstinence from food and fluids may remove the risk of gastrointestinal upset, factors such as glycogen levels, hunger and, most importantly, hydration must be taken into account.

Dietitians generally recommend the consumption of carbohydrate-rich meals no less than every two hours, and small amounts of fruit, carbohydrate-based drink or water in shorter breaks.

During the post-exercise period, glycogen restoration is most rapid and efficient, therefore the intake of foods that contain high GI levels such as sweets or fruit, sucrose or glucose, are vital for effective glycogen resynthesis. Although the player may not feel like eating much, if there is a delay in consumption, muscle glycogen recovery will be delayed, resulting in an incomplete replenishment of glycogen stores. Optimum recovery will result from the immediate replenishment of glycogen, followed by a high-carbohydrate meal within two to four hours.

FOOD AND FLUID INTAKE DURING COMPETITION

Food and drink consumed during exercise can enhance performance. It prevents changes to the body such as in the core temperature and a decrease in available muscle fuels. At least 75 per cent of the energy used whilst exercising is released as heat, with the evaporation of sweat being the most important mechanism for dissipating this and maintaining the body's thermal balance.

If fluid loss is greater than fluid intake, dehydration occurs. Buskirk and Puhl[3] state that when dehydration exceeds approximately 2 per cent of body weight, a decrease in performance becomes apparent. If 6–10 per cent of body weight is lost, then heat stroke and heat exhaustion becomes life threatening. For sporting events that last for 30–60 minutes, athletes should consider the benefits of consuming fluids during the event to reduce the chance of dehydration. During exercise, it is vital that food and drinks are appropriate and palatable to the athlete concerned: sweet or tepid substances are unlikely to be well tolerated.

Brouns et al[4] highlighted the issue of gastrointestinal comfort in sports performers. This is particularly relevant to high-intensity and high-impact movements where the athlete may the experience some 'joggling' of the gastric contents.

HYDRATION

The availability of adequate fluid is essential before, during and after exercise or competition. For badminton players exercising for periods of less than ninety minutes, regular water intake is sufficient, however, any player exceeding this may need carbo-hydrate-supplemented fluids to stay fully hydrated.

Fluids should be ingested as frequently as is practical and necessary for the individual, and in as large a volume as can be tolerated. Such fluids should be cooled to improve palata-bility and enhance body temperature control. Fluids should not be frozen. Drinks containing caffeine or alcohol are not ideal as they have a diuretic effect.

Nowadays, a wide range of sports drinks are available. Several studies have been conducted to test various combinations of fructose, glucose and glucose polymers in order to develop the optimum sports drink. However, scientific research indicates that the ideal fluid is simply a carbohydrate drink of 3–8 per cent concentration with the addition of a very small amount of sodium.

Recipes for Isotonic Drinks

50g (1¾oz) glucose or sugar
Pinch of salt
Low-sugar/low-calorie squash
1l warm water
Dissolve the sugar and salt in a little of the water. Allow to cool, cover and chill. Flavour with low-sugar or low-calorie squash to taste and top up with the remaining water.

Pinch of salt
500ml warm water
500ml unsweetened fruit juice
Dissolve the salt in a little of the water. Add the fruit juice and remaining water. Mix, cover and chill.

Pinch of salt
1l warm water
200ml squash

Dissolve the salt in a little of the water. Add the squash and remaining water. Mix, cover and chill.

Note: make up a new drink each day and don't keen any unused drink. Keep the bottle clean and never share it.

SUMMARY

Through a basic physiological understanding of the demands that badminton as a sport places upon them, players should be able to predict factors that are likely to negatively influence their performance and cause fatigue. With insight and forward planning, it is possible to prepare a schedule for food and fluid intake before, during and after exercise that will reduce or delay these effects.

While scientific recommendations form the basis for general guidelines, it should not be forgotten that some athletes not only tolerate but also often perform best on other feeding schedules. It is important that emphasis should be placed on the importance of trying out proposed competition food and fluid intake strategies.

REFERENCES

[1] Burke and Reid, 1989
[2] Burke, 1992
[3] Buskirk and Puhl
[4] Brouns *et al*

FURTHER READING

Burke, L. and Deakin, V., *Clinical Sports Nutrition* (McGraw Hill, 1994)
Paish, W., *Diet in Sport* (EP Publishing Ltd, 1979)

CHAPTER 9

Training

WARMING-UP FOR BADMINTON

There are a number of elements that a player needs to be able to master and perform during a game, and is essential that he warms up with these elements in mind. During a game, a badminton player will be required to demonstrate:

- agility;
- flexibility;
- power/strength;

- speed;
- footwork;
- reaction.

All of these elements must, however, be incorporated with a basic stamina to give a player sufficient durability for tournaments and tours. Dynamic warm-ups, specifically designed to get player's body ready for the demands of the game, are a modern method for warming-up and covering these elements.

An example of a dynamic warm-up for a badminton player would be as follows:

STAGE 1 Lift heart rate	Jogging for 1–2 minutes Skipping for 1–2 minutes
STAGE 2 Footwork	Zig-zag footwork movement (*see* page 75) Forward and reverse, 20m (22yd) both ways Leg cross-over – sideways and forward, 20m (22yd)
STAGE 3 Static stretches	All round body stretches: hamstrings, quads, triceps, shoulders
STAGE 4 Movement stretches	Jogging combined with arm stretches – single arm rotation and double arm rotation, 20m (22yd)
STAGE 5 Dynamic stretches	Walking lunges × 6, 20m (22yd); walking lunges with torso twist × 6 20m (22yd), backward lunges × 6, 20m (22yd)
STAGE 6 Dynamic stretches	Jogging, heel bottom kicks 20m (22yd), knee raises × 20m (22yd), hurdle action 20m (22yd), knee to shoulder twists
STAGE 7 Fast feet	Pattering – 4 second bursts, double feet pattering – 4 second bursts, sprint – jog burst 20m (22yd)
STAGE 8 Shadow play	Shadow movement on court – playing shadow shots 2 minutes on court

Fig 115 Walking leg lunges.

Fig 116 Forward leg lift.

Fig 117 Sideways leg lift.

Fig 118 High knee lift.

Fig 119 Butt kicks (heel bottom kicks).

Fig 120 Arm extensions, alternate arms.

Fig 121 Keyhole slaps.

FOOTWORK MOVEMENTS

These are just two examples of footwork movements that can be used by players as part of their warm-up routines. The aim, as for any warm-up routine, should be to concentrate on quality rather than quantity.

Zig-Zag Footwork

With the body facing forward, take two steps diagonally with the left leg leading, two steps with the right leg leading and then repeat. This is done at a jogging pace and the arms are used to help balance. Do not let the feet touch. Do this for two repetitions of 20m (22yd) forward and backward.

Leg Cross-Over

Start the movement sideways and take the right leg across the front of the left leg, then bring the left leg level again and take the right leg behind the back of the left. This should be done at jogging pace whilst using the arms to balance the body. Do this for three repetitions of 20m (22yd).

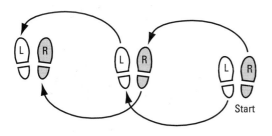

Fig 122 Foot positions for leg cross-overs.

WARMING DOWN

After playing a match or training it is important to warm down. This is the process of letting your body cool down and recover. The wrong thing to do is to just stop and do nothing: the body responds better if things are gradual. An example of this would be to walk around after running or gently jog, which slowly brings the heart rate down. Stretching the muscles after exercise forms part of the process of warming down as they have been active and had demands put on them. Always stretch the muscles that have been made to work, as this is a good way of dispersing any lactic acid that has been building up during exercise and can create cramp in muscles. Stretching muscles in the arms, legs and the body's trunk after exercise will also improve flexibility in a player. A good warm-down, lasting 5–15 minutes will prevent muscle fatigue and soreness.

STRETCHING EXERCISES TO IMPROVE FLEXIBILTY

Stretching should form part of any player's warm-up and training, as it conditions the body for strength and flexibility. Stretching, as part of a player's training, will help prevent injury during matches: it also can be used to improve footwork and agility during games. In order to maintain suppleness, stretching exercises must be performed both in and out of season.

Listed below are a number of basic exercises that all players would find useful to include as part of their stretching routine.

Shoulder and Chest Stretch

Place the arm over the head, hold the elbow with the opposite arm and gently pull across. Move the body in the direction of the pull, then repeat the movement for the other side of the body. Repeat three times on each side.

Fig 123 Shoulders and chest.

Fig 124 Hamstrings.

Arm and Shoulder Stretch

Place the arm over and behind the head, holding the elbow with the opposite arm. Gently push the elbow down, and hold. Repeat with the other arm. Repeat three times for each arm.

Hamstring Stretch

Stand with feet placed one in front of the other, bending the back leg but keeping the whole of the foot on the ground. Gently push

forward and down. The stretch should be felt in the front leg. Repeat with the other leg. Repeat three times for each leg.

Hip and Inner Thigh Stretch

1. Starting in the sitting position with legs spread out as wide as possible, bend gently forward, keeping the knees in a locked position. Slide both hands in front and use for support. Hold the stretch for 5 seconds then relax.

Fig 125 Arms and shoulders.

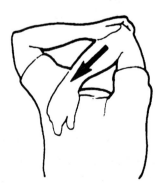

Fig 126 Groin, hips
and inner thighs.

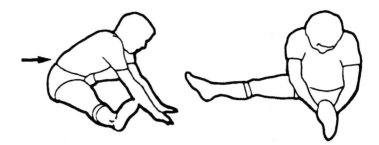

2. Place both hands on one leg under the knee and slide the leg down until the stretch can be felt. Hold the stretch for 3 seconds, then relax. Repeat for the other leg.

Groin Stretch

Starting in the sitting position, place the soles of the feet flat together and clasp the hands around the toes. Pull the feet towards the body and push down with the elbows at the sides of the knees. Hold for 5 seconds then relax. Repeat five times.

Fig 127 Groin.

Upper Body Twist and Stretch

Starting in the sitting position, place the left foot on the right side of the right knee. Place the back of the right elbow on the left-hand side of the left knee, which is now bent. Place the left hand on the floor to support the back. Push the left knee to the right with the right elbow whilst turning the head and shoulders to the left as far as possible. Hold for 5 seconds. Repeat with the right leg.

Fig 128 Spinal twist.

Hips and Quadriceps Stretch

Start with the right leg in front, with the right knee directly over the right ankle and the left knee touching the floor behind. Lower the hips, keeping them square to the floor. Make sure that both feet are in line and that the body is balanced, using both arms for stability. Hold for 3 seconds. Repeat with left leg.

Fig 129 Hips and quadriceps.

Calf and Achilles' Stretch

Start by standing facing a wall, leaning forward and supporting the body weight on the front arms. Place one leg in front of the other, keeping the back leg straight. Gently move the hips forward, keeping the back straight and both feet flat on the floor. In the same position, lower the hips and hold for five seconds. Repeat for other leg.

STRENGTH, SPEED AND AGILITY

Badminton is a sport that requires strength, speed and agility to develop explosive movement and hit with power and control.

Gains in strength may be made by using heavy weights with low repetitions and slow movements. Although strength is fundamental to any training programme, exercises should not be attempted in the absence of a qualified instructor. Speed and agility are, however, as important as strength, and much emphasis should be placed on developing these abilities on court.

Power

The ability to move powerfully and explosively on court is as important as being able to hit the shuttle powerfully. Training for power in badminton can be done in a number of different ways. Players may train using weights in exercises such as the

Fig 130 Calf and Achilles stretch.

overhead press, squats, and speed press-ups. These should all be done at maximum speed for six to eight repetitions per set with a full recovery between sets. The player's body needs to be fully recovered between sets to get the maximum benefit from the exercises.

Plyometric Jumping

This is an extremely important power movement in badminton. Whenever landing with plyometric jumps, the legs should be flexed to cushion and control the movement. Knees and hips should be well aligned to reduce the possibility of injury. In the event of injury, consult a physiotherapist.

The following exercises may be used to help condition the body for the use of plyometric movement during play:

- two-footed jumps forward – three sets of repetitions;
- side to side jumps over a bench – three sets of repetitions;
- long strides whilst running (like the triple jump movement) – three sets of repetitions;
- from a bench, jump off backwards, and immediately jump back on with feet at shoulder width apart – five sets of repetitions.

As with all plyometric jumping for exercise, the least amount of time spent on the ground between jumps, the better. It is important not to overdo it (the work to rest ratio should be a minimum of 1:6), and players should not attempt weights or plyometrics until they are physically mature.

REACTION WORK FOR BADMINTON PLAYERS

Badminton players require fast reactions to be able to cope with quick forecourt play and there are a number of exercises that can help improve and develop this ability.

- Player one gently throws a ball towards his partner who is facing in the opposite direction. Upon throwing the ball, the feeder calls to his partner to turn and try and

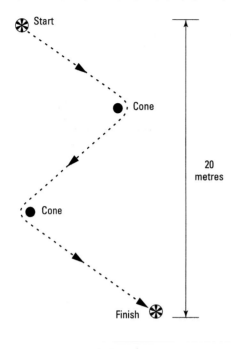

Fig 131 Diagonal sprint exercises.

catch the ball. To increase difficulty, the feeder can leave the call later and later. This improves hand and eye reactions. The use of a soft ball is recommended.

- Place bin bags or a sheet over the badminton net and play push shots from beneath the level of the net. Players cannot see the shuttle until it travels over the net. This improves reactions and is a good game.
- Standing forward with a person either side of the worker approx. 2m (6½ft) apart, the ball is dropped from one side or the other. Not knowing which side the ball will be dropped from, the worker has to react using peripheral vision, explosive movement and speed to catch the ball before it bounces for the second time.

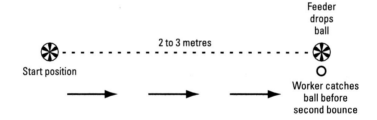

Fig 132 Forward sprint exercise.

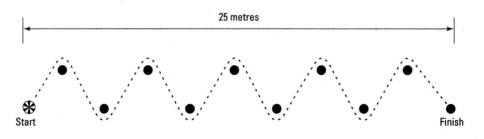

Fig 133 Sideways movement exercise worked at speed.

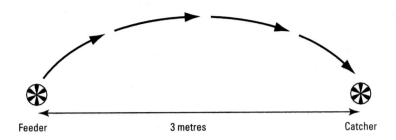

Fig 134 Turn and Catch – exercise.

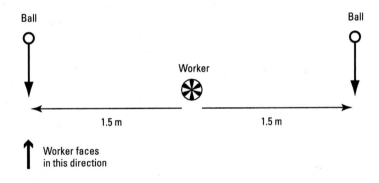

Fig 135 Reaction ball exercise for sideways movement.

SEASONAL TRAINING

Badminton can be broken down into seasons

● in season: September – May
● out of season: June – August

Stretching

In order to maintain suppleness, stretching exercises should be maintained throughout the year.

Agility and Speed

Out of season
● skipping
● balance
● coordination

Pre-season

● obstacle course
● skipping
● random agility exercises
● basic sprints

In season
● skipping
● random agility exercises
● sprints with multi-directional changes

Strength

Out of season   Maintain time to train and build strength for matches.

Pre-season   Maximum of one session per week.

Power

Pre-season   Specific power exercises that are closely linked with badminton requirements.

In season   Maintain basic exercises such as plyometrics.

Speed

Pre-season   Basic speed drills.

In season: Movement drills specific to badminton such as shuttle runs

FUN GAMES FOR CHILDREN

It is important that learning should be fun for children. There is nothing so boring as having to do the same thing over and over again. By playing fun, badminton-orientated games, it helps keep young minds interested as well as having a hidden agenda: coordination with hand, eye and racket; court awareness, agility and speed.

These games can be played on or off court – you can also make them up as you go along, but here are a few ideas.

King of the Court

One player stands in one half of the court, while the rest of the class stand at the back of the opposite side. Each player takes it in turn to beat the player who is on his own. If he wins the rally he wins a point and goes to the back of the queue until it is his turn to play again. A player becomes King of the Court when he has won three points against the existing 'king' and they then change places. The game starts again with all scores at zero.

Round The World – A Continuous Hit and Run Game

The player returns the shot to the feeder then runs around the outside of the court and back to the start. If the player makes a mistake he 'loses a life'. If he loses two lives, he is 'out'. When only two players are left they become the winners. The game gets harder when fewer players are left.

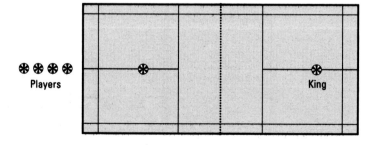

Fig 136 King of the Court – a children's game.

Players

King

Tag Badminton

Split the class into two equal teams and stand each team at the back of the court on either side. The first players from each side move on to court to take the first shot, they move off to allow their next team-mate to play the next shot and so on until the point is won or lost. Play the game like a match up to 15 points.

Penalties

During a rally on court, if a player misses the shuttle he has to stand on one leg as a penalty. The penalties for missing consecutive shots are: kneeling down, sitting, and lying. If he misses the next shot, he is out.

However, if he returns the shuttle, he goes back to his previous position:

- lying – back to sitting;
- sitting – back to kneeling;
- kneeling – back to one leg;
- one leg – back to normal standing.

TARGETS

It is always a good idea to give children incentives, and putting targets in areas where you want them to hit the shuttle is a good idea. I like to use hoops placed in certain areas to practise shots such as high and low service, drop shots, clears and net shots. The targets can be moved to hit around the court and points can be awarded for landing the shuttle in the hoop.

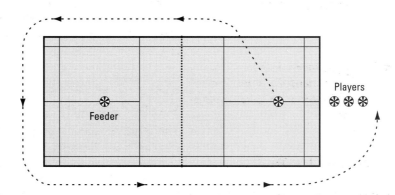

Fig 137 Round the World – a children's game.

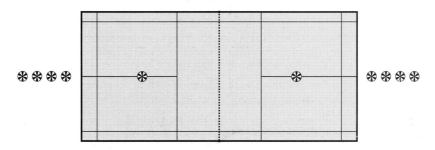

Fig 138 Tag Badminton – a children's game.

CHAPTER 10

The Road to Success

THE BEGINNER TO JUNIOR INTERNATIONAL

Schools are full of children who play badminton, but only very few find they have a real talent for the sport and look to join a junior badminton club. The promising club player then looks to the town or junior county team, which offers not just the chance to play at a higher standard, but coaches who are able to develop a player's natural ability and help him to master the finer points of the game. With the correct coaching, a player will develop very quickly, and, with the encouragement of the coach, will begin to enter local tournaments. It is at this point that badminton changes from being just a game to become a competitive sport.

All children love winning but they also have to come to terms with losing and how to handle it. Some players just shrug off defeat, but others get upset, cry and often throw tantrums. An understanding coach or parent is the key here – a few carefully chosen words can turn defeat into a chance to do better next time.

Once a junior begins to enter tournaments, he should start to prepare for matches. Looking at the opposition's strengths and weaknesses is the first step to becoming tactically aware.

Many juniors do not wish to or cannot progress beyond this point, however if a player does decide to continue, there are plenty of opportunities for young players to start to climb the ladder of success within the badminton world.

Coaching cells are set up regionally but only a select few are offered places to attend. Alongside the regional cells or squads, there are national training weekends where players are invited to play and learn from highly qualified coaches. This is the start of the long process of learning about diet, nutrition, movement skills, training procedures and how to cope during matches and tournaments played at home or abroad.

Once a player is selected to attend coaching cells or training weekends, he will be required to improve his fitness levels and maintain them at the highest standard. This may mean training up to four times a week plus on-court practices. Badminton is one of the most physically demanding sports and a successful player must work hard on and off court.

As a player grows older, normal teenage activities start to interfere but players who wish to succeed in badminton need to make a choice. It is vital that the right mix is found between working, playing badminton and other activities. If the mix is wrong, it can

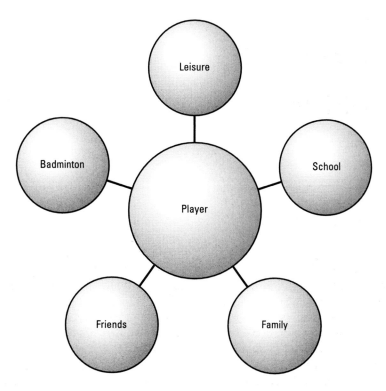

Fig 139 A player's bubble diagram showing elements in their life.

have a negative effect on the player: too much of one thing or too little can affect other areas. Talking to a coach or a player with experience is important. If the right mix is found, then the badminton will flourish and a player will be happy to continue.

However, as a player gets older some elements of the mix may change, becoming either more or less important – some elements may disappear completely and be replaced by something totally new. For example, a player may leave school and concentrate on badminton; the school bubble would then go and the badminton bubble would get larger. All players must be aware that devoting oneself exclusively to a main objective can sometimes fail because the overall balance is wrong. This is why it is always important to take advice from successful athletes, whatever their sport.

A player will mature, mentally and physically, becoming more independent and less reliant on others to tell him what to do. This is an important development if a player is to make it as a top-class player as he must be:

- 100 per cent willing to do what is requested of him;
- 100 per cent focused on what he is doing;
- able to listen and learn;
- able to find the right balance of hard work and enjoyment;
- disciplined and reliable;
- determined to succeed.

JUNIOR INTERNATIONAL TO SENIOR INTERNATIONAL

This should be treated as a gradual move towards the senior game and not a quick jump. The transition can be very difficult as a top junior player will have become used to winning in his respective age group, but must now encounter senior players who have much greater experience and knowledge. Inevitably, this can cause problems with confidence and attitude.

An experienced coach can save the situation as he can advise on the best tournaments to play, which will help build confidence and develop experience. A number of juniors now have the chance to train with the seniors on a regular basis; providing an ideal opportunity for the up-and-coming player to be with his role models on court.

This step up to the senior level will mean a complete change in lifestyle for all young players, as they will be expected to move away from home to a training base. This will mean having to think for themselves and not rely on others to have the all the answers or help motivate them to train.

ESSENTIAL QUALITIES AND ATTRIBUTES

The successful transition from being a junior player to a top senior international relies on a number of key factors. In addition to hard work, determination and dedication, the player must also have the vision to know what he wants and the right mental attitude to succeed in achieving it

Communication

This is important for all top sports performers. Without the ability to communicate clearly, it is extremely difficult for others to help. Top international players are sometimes thrown into the public eye and being able to communicate in an articulate manner is important.

However, it is equally important for a player be able to listen and interpret information correctly. A player will have to work with managers, coaches, doctors and their own playing partners. The team surrounding the player is vital to his success, therefore the ability to communicate and work together is essential.

Self-Confidence

The player's belief that he can consistently perform at a high level not only encourages partners and team mates, but can also work to demoralize the opposition.

Education

A player has to be able to learn both from experience of the game, and from assimilating the advice and information gained through working with psychologists and coaches.

It is important that a young player does not neglect his schoolwork and examinations. A sporting career is relatively short-lived and a player is likely to need academic qualifications to enable him to find employment once his playing career has finished.

Finance

Although a player will play for the love of the game, he cannot survive on it alone. A player who wishes to succeed will require some form of financial assistance. The help provided by sponsors and local government in the form of grants, prize money and exhibition fees will form part of a player's financial existence,

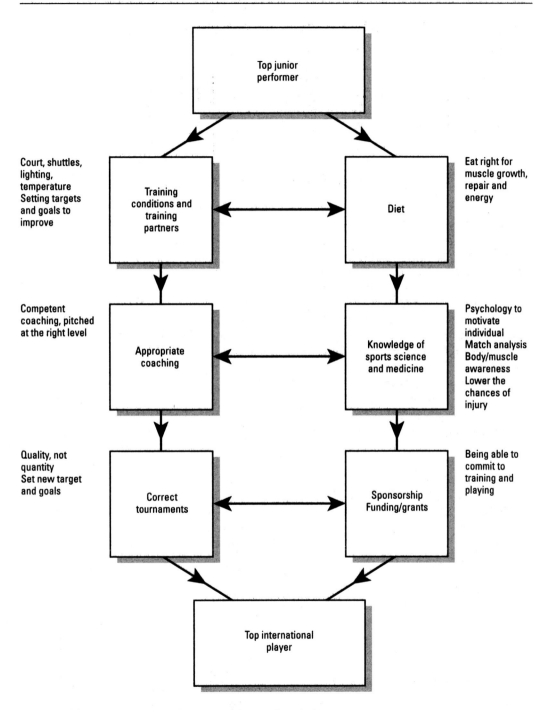

Fig 140 The transition from junior to international player.

without which it would be impossible to train and travel to tournaments to play.

Lifestyle Management

The ability to plan a lifestyle to produce the correct mix of training, playing, travel, recreation, family and friends produces a well-balanced player who can cope with all eventualities

TOP INTERNATIONAL TO WORLD-CLASS PLAYER

Once the step has been made from junior to senior international there is only one more rung on the ladder to go, which is from top senior international to world-class player – the type of player who will be top seed in any Grand Prix tournament. As badminton has recently been recognized as an Olympic sport, players can now also aspire to becoming an Olympian or Evan medallist and gaining global recognition.

A world-class player must have achieved the right level of ability and consistency between the ages of nineteen and twenty-four. Between the ages of twenty-five to twenty-nine he will have established his dominance in the game and reaped the rewards of success in tournaments and international appearances.

For a player to become a world-class act he must be able to cope with the day-to-day pressure that this would involve – a player's mental approach is the key to success. Badminton is not such a high-profile sport as, for example, tennis or football, however, a player must still handle himself in the correct manner. It is this composure and confidence that can make the difference between being an international or a world-class player.

Rules of Badminton

DEFINITIONS

Player	Any person playing badminton.
Match	The basic contest in badminton between opposing sides, each of one or two players.
Singles	A match where there is one player on each of the opposing sides.
Doubles	A match where there are two players on each of the opposing sides.
Serving side	The side having the right to serve.
Receiving side	The side opposing the serving side.

THE COURT AND COURT EQUIPMENT

Lines

The court shall be a rectangle laid out with lines 40mm wide.

The lines shall be easily distinguishable and preferably be coloured white or yellow.

All lines form part of the area which they define.

Posts

The posts shall be 1.55m in height from the surface of the court and shall remain vertical when the net is strained between both posts.

The posts shall be placed on the doubles sidelines irrespective of whether singles or doubles is being played.

Net

The net shall be made of fine, dark-coloured cord and of even thickness with a mesh of not less than 15mm and not more than 20mm.

The net shall be 760mm in depth and at least 6.1m wide.

The top of the net shall be edged with a 75mm white cloth tape doubled over a cord or cable running through the tape. This tape must rest upon the cord or cable.

The cord or cable shall be stretched firmly, flush with the top of the posts.

The top of the net from the surface of the court shall be 1.5m at the centre of the court and 1.524m over the sidelines for doubles.

There shall be no gaps between the ends of the net and the posts. If necessary, the full depth of the net should be tied at the ends.

SHUTTLE

The shuttle may be made from natural and/or synthetic materials. From whatever material the shuttle is made, the flight characteristics generally should be similar to those produced by a natural feathered shuttle with a cork base covered by a thin layer of leather.

The shuttle shall have sixteen feathers fixed in the base.

The feathers shall be measured from the tip to the top of the base and shall be of the same length in each shuttle. This length should be 62–70mm.

The tips of the feathers shall lie on a circle with a diameter of 58–68mm.

The feathers shall be fastened firmly with thread or other suitable material.

The base shall be 25–28mm in diameter and rounded on the bottom.

The shuttle shall weigh from 4.74–5.50 grams.

Non-Feathered Shuttle

The skirt, or simulation of feathers in synthetic materials, replaces natural feathers.

Testing a Shuttle for Speed

To test a shuttle, use a full underhand stroke that makes contact with the shuttle over the back boundary line. The shuttle should be hit at an upward angle and in a direction parallel to the sidelines.

A shuttle of correct speed will land not less than 530mm and not more than 990mm short of the other back boundary line.

RACKET

The racket shall be free of:

- attached objects and protrusions, other than those used solely and specifically to limit or prevent wear and tear, or vibration, or to distribute weight, or to secure the handle by cord to the player's hand, and which are reasonable in size and placement for such purposes;

- any device which makes it possible for a player to change materially the shape of the racket.

The main racket parts are called the handle, the stringed area, the head, the shaft, the throat and the frame:

- the handle is the part of the racket intended to be gripped by the player;
- the stringed area is the part of the racket with which it is intended the player hits the shuttle;
- the head bounds the stringed area;
- the shaft connects the handle to the head;
- the throat (if present) connects the shaft to the head;
- the frame is the name given to the head, throat, shaft and handle taken together. The frame of the racket shall not exceed 680mm in overall length and 230mm in overall width.

Stringed Area

The stringed area shall be flat and consist of a pattern of crossed strings. The stringing pattern shall be generally uniform and, in particular, not less dense in the centre than in any other area.

The stringed area shall not exceed 280mm in overall length and 220mm in overall width. However, the strings may extend into an area which otherwise would be the throat, provided that the width of the extended stringed area does not exceed 35mm and the overall length does not then exceed 330mm.

TOSS

Before play commences, a toss shall be conducted and the side winning the toss can then choose to do one of the following:

- to serve or receive first; or
- to start play at one end of the court or the other.

The side losing the toss shall then exercise the remaining choice.

SCORING SYSTEM

A match shall consist of the best of three games, unless otherwise arranged.

In doubles and men's singles, the first side to score 15 points, except when setting, wins the game.

In ladies' singles, the first side to score 11 points, except when setting, wins the game.

If the score becomes 14-all (10-all in ladies' singles), the side which first scored 14 (10) can decide:

- to continue the game to 15 (11) points, i.e. not to set the game; or
- to set the game to 17 (13) points.

The side winning a game serves first in the next game.

Only the serving side can add a point to its score.

The following rules are likely to come into effect in May 2002:

- All games are to be scored and played as the best of 5 games to 7 points. In the event of the score being 6 points all, then the side who reached 6 first has the choice to (i) continue to seven points, or (ii) set to 8 points.
- Players shall change ends after each game, and in the fifth game (if any) when the leading score reaches 4 points. There is a 90-second break allowed between games in all matches.

CHANGE OF ENDS

Players shall change ends:

- at the end of the first game;
- prior to the beginning of the third game (if any);
- in the third game, or in a match of one game, when the leading score reaches:

6 in a game of 11 points; or
8 in a game of 15 points.

If players forget to change ends, they shall do so as soon as the mistake is discovered and the shuttle is not in play. The existing score shall stand.

SERVICE

In a correct service:

- neither side shall cause undue delay to the delivery of the service once the server and receiver have taken up their respective positions;
- the server and receiver shall stand within diagonally opposite service courts without touching the boundary lines;
- some part of both feet of the server and receiver must remain in contact with the surface of the court in a stationary position from the start of the service until the service is delivered;
- the server's racket shall initially hit the base of the shuttle; it is a fault to hit the feathers first;
- the whole shuttle shall be below the server's waist at the instant of being hit by the server's racket;
- the shaft of the server's racket at point of contact with the shuttle has to be visibly below the racket hand;

- the movement of the server's racket must continue forward after the start of the service until the service is delivered – it is not allowed to stop or move backward again;
- the shuttle has to be hit over the net and into the receiver's service court.

If any of the above are performed incorrectly, it is a fault.

Once the players have taken their positions, the first forward movement of the server's racket head is the start of the service.

The server shall not serve before the receiver is ready but the receiver shall be considered to have been ready if a return of service is attempted.

In doubles, the partners may take up any positions that do not unsight or put off the opposing server or receiver.

SINGLES

Serving and Receiving Courts

The players shall serve from the right-hand service court when they are at an even number or when no points have been scored.

The players shall serve from the left-hand service court when they are at an odd number.

The shuttle is hit alternately by the server and the receiver until a fault is made or the shuttle ceases to be in play.

Scoring and Serving

If the receiver makes a fault, or the shuttle ceases to be in play because it touches the surface of the court inside the receiver's court, the server scores a point. The server then serves again from the other service court.

If the server makes a fault, or the shuttle ceases to be in play because it touches the surface of the court inside the server's court,

the server loses the right to continue serving and the receiver then becomes the server, with no point scored by either player.

DOUBLES

At the start of a game, and each time a side gains the right to serve, the service has to be played from the right-hand service court.

Only the receiver shall return the service: if the shuttle is touched or hit by the receiver's partner, it is a fault and the serving side scores a point.

Order of Play and Position on Court

After the service is returned, the shuttle may be hit by either player of the serving side and then by either player of the receiving side and so on, until the shuttle ceases to be in play.

After the service is returned, a player may hit the shuttle from any position on that player's side of the net.

Scoring and Serving

If the receiving side makes a fault or the shuttle ceases to be in play because it touches the surface of the court inside the receiving side's court, the serving side scores a point and the server serves again.

If the serving side makes a fault, or the shuttle ceases to be in play because it touches the surface of the court inside the serving side's court, the server loses the right to continue serving, with no point scored by either side.

Serving and Receiving Courts

The player who serves at the start of any game shall serve from, or receive in, the right-hand service court when that player's side has not scored or has scored an even number of points in that game, and the left-hand service court when that player's side has scored an odd number of points. The reverse pattern shall apply to partners.

Service in any turn of serving shall be delivered from alternate service courts.

During any game, the right to serve passes from one side to the other when both pairs have served and lost the rallies. The serve then starts with the player in the right-hand service box and then on to their partner if the rally is lost, then to the opposition if the serving team loses that rally.

No player shall serve out of turn, receive out of turn, or receive two consecutive services in the same game.

Either player of the winning side may serve first in the next game, and either player of the losing side may receive.

SERVICE COURT ERRORS

A service court error has been made when a player:

- has served out of turn;
- has served from the wrong service court; or
- is standing in the wrong service court, was prepared to receive the service and it has been delivered.

If a service court error is discovered after the next service has been delivered, the error shall not be corrected.

If a service court error is discovered before the next service is delivered:

- if both sides committed an error, it shall be a let;
- if one side committed the error and won the rally, it shall be a let;

- if one side committed the error and lost the rally, the error shall not be corrected.

If there is a let because of a service court error, the rally is replayed with the error corrected.

If a service court error is not to be corrected, play in that game shall proceed without changing the players' new service courts (nor, when relevant, the new order of serving).

FAULTS

It is a fault if a service is not correct (*see* pages 91–92).

It is a fault if, in play, the shuttle lands:

- outside the boundaries of the court (not on or within the boundary lines);
- passes through or under the net;
- fails to pass the net;
- touches the ceiling or sidewalls;
- touches the person or dress of a player;
- touches any other object or person outside the immediate surroundings of the court;

  (Where an obstacle such as a beam or light fitting is overhanging a court area then this may be deemed a let during play. This is normally agreed before the start of a match.)

- if, when in play, the initial point of contact with the shuttle is not on the striker's side of the net.

  (The striker may, however, follow the shuttle over the net with the racket in the course of a stroke.)

It is a fault if, when the shuttle is in play, a player:

- touches the net or its supports with racket, person or dress;
- invades an opponent's court over the net with racket or person except when following through with a stroke;
- invades an opponent's court under the net with racket or person such that an opponent is obstructed or distracted;
- obstructs or prevents an opponent from making a legal stroke where the shuttle is followed over the net;
- deliberately distracts an opponent by any action such as shouting or making gestures;

It is a fault if, in play, the shuttle:

- is caught and held on the racket and then slung during the execution of a stroke;
- is hit twice in succession by the same player with two strokes;
- is hit by a player and the player's partner successively;
- touches a player's racket and continues towards the back of that player's court.
- is caught on the net on service and remains suspended on top or, on service, after passing over, is then caught in the net.

LETS

'Let' is called by the umpire, or by a player (if there is no umpire), to halt play.

A let may be given for any unforeseen or accidental occurrence.

It shall be a let if:

- a shuttle is caught on the net and remains suspended on top or, after passing over the net, is caught in the net, it shall be a let except on service.

- during service, the receiver and server are both faulted at the same time;
- the server serves before the receiver is ready;
- the shuttle disintegrates and the base completely separates from the rest of the shuttle;
- a line judge is unsighted and the umpire is unable to make a decision.

When a let occurs, the play since the last service shall not count and the player who served shall serve again.

SHUTTLE NOT IN PLAY

A shuttle is not in play when:

- it strikes the net and remains attached there or suspended on top;
- it strikes the net or post and starts to fall towards the surface of the court on the striker's side of the net;
- it hits the surface of the court;
- a fault or let has occurred.

CONTINUOUS PLAY, MISCONDUCT, PENALTIES

Play shall be continuous from the first service until the match is concluded, except as allowed by an umpire or referee.

Intervals not exceeding 90 seconds between the first and second games, and not exceeding 5 minutes between the second and third games, are allowed in all matches in international competitive events, IBF-sanctioned events, and all other matches unless the member association has previously published a decision not to allow such intervals.

Suspension of Play

When necessitated by circumstances not within the control of the players, the umpire may suspend play for such a period as the umpire may consider necessary.

Under special circumstances the referee may instruct the umpire to suspend play.

If play is suspended, the existing score shall stand and play shall be resumed from that point.

Under no circumstances shall play be delayed to enable a player to recover strength or wind.

COACHING ADVICE AND LEAVING THE COURT

Except in the intervals where applicable, no player shall be permitted to receive coaching advice during a match.

Except during the five-minute interval, no player shall leave the court during a match

without the umpire's permission.

The umpire shall be the sole judge of any delay in play.

A player shall not:

- deliberately cause delay in, or suspension of, play;
- deliberately modify or damage the shuttle in order to change its speed or its flight;
- behave in an offensive manner.

GAMES OF OTHER THAN 11 OR 15 POINTS

It is permissible to play one game of 21 points by prior arrangement. In this case the following variations apply:

- setting is permitted at 20-all and then only to 23 points;
- players must change ends when the leading score reaches 11 points.

USEFUL ADDRESSES

Badminton Association of England
National Badminton Centre
Loughton Lodge
Milton Keynes
Buckinghamshire MK8 9LA

International Badminton Federation
Manor Park Place
Rutherford Way
Cheltenham
Gloucestershire GL51 9TU

Badminton Union of Ireland
Terenure Badminton Centre
Whitehall Road
Dublin 12
Republic of Ireland

Welsh Badminton Union
Head Office
4th Floor
Plymouth Chambers
8 Westgate Street
Cardiff
CF10 1DP

Scottish Badminton Union
Cockburn Centre
40 Bogmoor Place
Glasgow
G51 4TQ

www.badmintoncoaching.com
A good coaching website.

Index